Praise fo

Dean is a courageous leader who: book. With refreshing bluntness, he pulls no punches as he lovingly confronts the false assurances our enemy lures us toward. After you finish this book, you'll find yourself sharing it with others!

J. D. GREEAR
President of the Southern Baptist Convention

At first glance, *The Unsaved Christian* seems to be a classic oxymoron. But when Dean Inserra unpacks the reality of cultural Christianity today, he hits us right between the eyes with the state of much of Christianity we see in our communities and our churches. This book is practical. This book is pertinent. This book is powerful. I have already begun recommending it.

THOM S. RAINER
Founder and CEO, Church Answers
Author, *I Am a Church Member*

Cultural Christianity has been a popular target of critique for some time, but Dean offers us more than insight into its existence—he offers a way forward. Bringing pastoral and practical wisdom to the task, he coaches us on how to draw those with only a surface commitment to Christianity into true belief. *The Unsaved Christian* offers much-needed actionable help to the minister and the layperson alike.

JEN WILKIN
Author and Bible teacher

I am convinced that the greatest threat to the church today is not secularism or atheism, but nominal, cultural Christianity. An almost-gospel is worse than no gospel at all. A cultural Christianity sends its adherents to the same place that outright rejection of the gospel does, to hell, but pretends to put into the mouth of Jesus the old lie of the snake, "You shall not surely die." As the pastor of one of the most dynamic, growing, and gospel-centered churches in the country, Dean Inserra is well-qualified to equip the church on how to reach unsaved "Christians" with the only message that can really save: the gospel of Jesus Christ.

RUSSELL MOORE
President, The Ethics & Religious Liberty Commission of the Southern Baptist Convention

I know of few, if any, people who understand the gospel and evangelism in the middle of cultural Christianity more than Dean Inserra. This book is a reflection of both Dean's wisdom and experience. If you care about those who are cultural Christians, and want to be better equipped to share the gospel with them, you need this book.

MICAH FRIES
Pastor of Brainerd Baptist Church, Chattanooga, TN

One of the top young pastors in America has written a book that is both candid and courageous and tackles a subject that should make everyone who claims to be a "Christian" wake up, sit up, and listen up. One of the greatest threats to Christianity in America is cultural Christianity, and it may be the most popular—and dangerous—type of Christianity practiced in America, particularly and especially in the Bible Belt. The apostle Paul said "Examine yourselves, to see whether you are in the faith" (2 Cor. 13:5 ESV). This book will drive you to do just that and help you see whether or not you are ready for the final exam.

JAMES MERRITT
Pastor of Cross Pointe Church, Duluth, GA
Former President of the Southern Baptist Convention

Having been raised in an environment of cultural Christianity, it wasn't until I was a freshman in college that I truly experienced the life-changing power of a relationship with Jesus through the gospel. I now experience life and pastoring a church in Las Vegas, Nevada. Having lived through two extremes on this issue, I so appreciate Dean Inserra tackling this subject and providing such powerful insights. I thank God for Dean and the voice God has given him to speak into this generation so powerfully. We need an awakening in our nation, and it will begin in the church with a true movement to the gospel-centeredness. I highly recommend this book!

VANCE PITMAN
Senior Pastor of Hope Church, Las Vegas, NV

In this book, you will find that Dean's strong challenge to reach and disciple "cultural Christians" is coupled with great wisdom and insight. Dean has acquired that wisdom and insight by doing the hard work of ministry and effectively taking the gospel to "cultural Christians." If you serve in a context where people claim to be Christian because of their church affiliation or family, you should read this book.

ERIC GEIGER
Senior Pastor of Mariners Church, Irvine, CA

When I ask myself where will we find the next generation of strong and effective leaders for the church, I think of Dean Inserra. He is thinking not just about the lost but the lost within the church. I'm a big fan, and I like this book.

JOHN W. YATES II
Senior Rector, The Falls Church Anglican

Dean Inserra's ministry shows the fruit of two unique passions—a deep conviction to challenge nominal, cultural Christianity, and a deep love for nominal, cultural "unsaved Christians." Dean and City Church embody the heart of Jesus that would rebuke the false religion of the Pharisee and yet weep over Jerusalem. As a pastor, *The Unsaved Christian* freshly challenged me. Do I love people enough to "help them get lost" so they can find the true grace of Jesus in the gospel?

MARK VANCE
Lead Pastor of Cornerstone Church, Ames, IA

THE

UNSAVED
CHRISTIAN

REACHING CULTURAL
CHRISTIANITY
WITH THE GOSPEL

DEAN INSERRA

MOODY PUBLISHERS
CHICAGO

© 2019 by
Dean Inserra

Unless otherwise noted, all Scripture quotations are taken from the Christian Standard Bible®, Copyright © 2017 by Holman Bible Publishers. Used by permission. Christian Standard Bible® and CSB® are federally registered trademarks of Holman Bible Publishers.

Scripture quotations marked esv are from the ESV® Bible (The Holy Bible, English Standard Version®), copyright © 2001 by Crossway, a publishing ministry of Good News Publishers. Used by permission. All rights reserved.

Scripture quotations marked niv are taken from the Holy Bible, New International Version®, NIV®. Copyright © 1973, 1978, 1984, 2011 by Biblica, Inc.™ Used by permission of Zondervan. All rights reserved worldwide. www.zondervan.com The "NIV" and "New International Version" are trademarks registered in the United States Patent and Trademark Office by Biblica, Inc.™

Some names and details have been changed to protect the privacy of individuals.

Published in association with the literary agent of Wolgemuth & Associates.

Edited by Connor Sterchi
Interior design: Ragont Design
Cover design: Erik M. Peterson

Library of Congress Cataloging-in-Publication Data

Names: Inserra, Dean, author.
Title: The unsaved Christian : reaching cultural Christianity with the Gospel / Dean Inserra.
Description: Chicago : Moody Publishers, 2019. | Includes bibliographical references.
Identifiers: LCCN 2018060950 (print) | LCCN 2019007429 (ebook) | ISBN 9780802497529 (ebook) | ISBN 9780802418807
Subjects: LCSH: Good works (Theology) | Christianity and culture. | Assurance (Theology) | Salvation--Christianity. | Evangelistic work.
Classification: LCC BT773 (ebook) | LCC BT773 .I57 2019 (print) | DDC 269/.2--dc23
LC record available at https://lccn.loc.gov/2018060950

ISBN: 978-0-8024-1880-7

We hope you enjoy this book from Moody Publishers. Our goal is to provide high-quality, thought-provoking books and products that connect truth to your real needs and challenges. For more information on other books and products written and produced from a biblical perspective, go to www.moodypublishers.com or write to:

Moody Publishers
820 N. LaSalle Boulevard
Chicago, IL 60610

5 7 9 10 8 6 4

Printed in the United States of America

To Karen Knox, who reached me
as an unsaved Christian.
May others be reached because of your efforts.

Contents

Preface

This book is for pastors, church leaders, and Christians living on mission. In the pages of this book, you will find a comprehensive overview of *cultural Christianity* and learn how Christians can spot and counter it with truth. America is the land of the over-churched and under-reached, and churches must understand that everything from church membership criteria, holiday services, Vacation Bible School, and other typical American church programming can either foster cultural Christianity or cripple it. Throughout this book, we'll come back to the simple principle that gospel clarity is the antidote to the rampant confusion: the gospel shows that God makes the demands, meets them in Christ, and then calls people to trust in and follow Him.

For the purposes of this book, I will consider people in terms of general groupings, though this is not to imply that real, individual people can be reached by a one-size-fits-all method or formula. The groupings in this book (generational Catholics, God & Country Christians, etc.) exist primarily to illustrate common ways people may place faith in a false gospel and still identify themselves as Christians. As the focus of this book is cultural Christianity, I will primarily focus on those who think they are fine with God because they have familiarity with Christian things.

Further, the primary objective of this book is to call Christians to action, especially church leaders who may realize that they have inadvertently allowed cultural Christianity to go unchallenged in their churches. I am, of course, in complete need of God's grace in all areas of my life. We all have a propensity to be attracted to lesser versions of the gospel—may this book point us to Jesus Christ so we can remain humble and wise. None of what follows is intended to disparage falsely assured believers but rather to expose the great mission field before us and caution fellow Christians to get serious about the gospel and proclaim the good news unapologetically. It truly is the power of God for salvation for all who would believe.

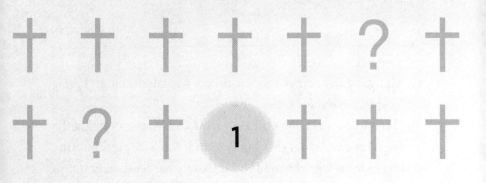

Help Them Get Lost:

The Case for Reaching Cultural Christians

Thinking that I deserve heaven is a sure sign
I have no understanding of the gospel.
—SINCLAIR FERGUSON

If there is such a thing as missional insecurity, I have felt it. It's that feeling you had in college when your friends spent spring break serving in a Haitian orphanage while you drove to the beach. My most vivid experience of this insecurity came while moving out of my seminary apartment. I was loading up to make the drive back to my hometown of Tallahassee, where I would begin local church pastoral ministry. I was excited to be heading home, until I saw my neighbor from our seminary apartment complex, Matt. He was moving to Northern California to join the staff of a local church. *Great*, I thought. *There's Matt packing up his family and entire life to move to one of the most secularized regions in America, and I am going back home, where I will live ten miles from the Georgia state line and less than an hour from Alabama. He's going on mission, I'm headed to the Bible Belt.*

I felt like I was taking the easy road and Matt was taking the courageous one, leading his family to an area where preaching the gospel of Jesus Christ would be just barely harder than finding a Republican. I was heading to the Land of the Monogrammed. I wanted to say something spiritual to make myself feel better. With the standard one-arm man hug, I said, "I really admire what you're doing and will pray for you as you head to an area with such an important Great Commission need."

Matt's reply was not what I was expecting.

"Whatever," he said, doing the required pat-on-the-back during our man hug, "the Bible Belt is the most difficult place in America to pastor a local church."

I was stunned. He must have sensed my confusion because he explained further. As he did, I had a serious epiphany. I believe the Lord knew what I needed to hear in that moment, and it changed my perspective forever on my role as a pastor in the part of the country where I live and minister. "In California," Matt said, "there is rarely confusion. Either you're a Christian or you're not. In the Bible Belt, many people think they're Christians but have no concept of the severity of sin, necessity of repentance, message of grace, or the overall message of the gospel. They think they're just fine with God and God is fine with them because they aren't atheists and have been to church before as a kid. It's almost like you have to help them get lost, so they can actually be saved. They believe in God, but do not believe their sin has done anything to separate them from Him or caused them to need the Jesus they claim to believe in."

You have to get them lost before they can actually be saved.

People are too quick to claim something is "life-changing,"

and I've done that myself about a new flavor of Blue Bell Ice Cream or some Kansas City BBQ. But from a ministry perspective, this really was the moment for me. The reality of Matt's description of my hometown created a missional urgency rather than missional insecurity. Since that parking lot conversation, I moved back home just south of the Georgia line to plant a church among people with Southern accents, who never missed Vacation Bible School as kids, and now drop their own kids off several weeks of the summer to different VBS programs across town. Whereas church familiarity is a rarity where Matt is, people back home will dress up to go to church on Easter Sunday, while having no concept of why that holiday even matters on Monday morning.

Since that conversation in our seminary apartment parking lot, I have also come to realize that the spiritual landscape Matt was describing is not unique to the South. What he was describing was *Cultural Christianity*: a religion that, I believe, is practiced by more Americans than any other faith or religion. Its participants can be found in Catholic or Protestant churches, in the South and Midwest, on high school football fields, at patriotic celebrations, and around family dinner tables. It looks and sounds very Christian on the surface, but is merely Christian by culture, rather than conviction. The gospel of Jesus Christ is not part of the equation.

The people who practice cultural Christianity are not atheists or agnostics. In fact, Cultural Christians would be offended if described with such labels. These are not the urban academics living in loft apartments who could articulate their opposition to Christian beliefs. These are the suburban, cul-de-sac folks hosting a cookout to watch the game. They believe in God. They take seriously their "Christian" traditions, prayer in schools, nativity scenes, and Linus reciting the story of the birth of Christ during *A Charlie Brown Christmas*.

> **Cultural Christianity admires Jesus, but doesn't really think He is needed, except to "take the wheel" in a moment of crisis.**

What is wrong with being a monotheist who loves Charlie Brown and believes Jesus was born in a manger? Nothing, if it leads to gospel belief and practice. But the difficulty comes when we examine exactly who their God is and question why the coming of Jesus even matters.

Cultural Christianity admires Jesus, but doesn't really think He is needed, except to "take the wheel" in a moment of crisis. The Jesus of Cultural Christianity is a type of historical imaginary friend with some magic powers for good luck and sentimentality. "Amazing Grace" is a song known from memory, but why that grace is amazing cannot be explained. The God of Cultural Christianity is the "big man upstairs," and whether or not He is holy and people have sinned against Him is irrelevant. Words such as "hope," "faith," and "believe" hang on the walls of living rooms as decorations, but the actual words of God only come around when Psalm 23 is read at a loved one's funeral.

Religious but Not Saved

It is well documented that those who claim no religious affiliation (called "the nones") are on the rise.[1] Between 2007 and 2014, the group of people self-identifying as having no religious affiliation jumped from 16.1 to 22.8 percent of the American population.[2] This coincides with a decline in people identifying as Christian, although there is reason to believe this is really just a refinement process and not a sign of bleeding in the actual Christian demographic. As the social costs of Christianity increase, those with only nominal belief are falling away.[3] According to a study of US adults, 80% of those polled believe in God, but only 56% believe in God as described in the Bible.[4] Considering the fact that approximately 70% of the US population still identifies as Christian, we have a large group of people that would likely be overlooked in outreach or missions. With this in mind, I believe Cultural Christianity is the most underrated mission field in America. While there is evidence that nominal Christianity is declining on its own, it is of utmost importance that we minister to those on the fence, in hopes that they may end up within the fold and not without.

The words my friend Matt used to challenge me in that parking lot have been confirmed since I moved back home to pastor in a city saturated with Cultural Christianity. Indeed, there is familiarity with church and Christian lingo, but a familiarity with the gospel is hard to find. To add to the problem, the church often "assumes the gospel." As a result, people can camp out in churches for years and never hear what the Bible actually says. What an opportunity to make a Great Commission impact! But Matt was right when he said it was difficult. Reaching people who think they are fine is a seldom-discussed starting point for evangelism and local church ministry.

Getting someone who thinks he's a Christian to see that he is actually *not* is a delicate and sensitive endeavor, but not unique to our time. Jesus Himself, in the greatest sermon ever preached, reminds us that being religious but not saved is not unique to our day. The Sermon on the Mount is our starting point for understanding Cultural Christianity, where Jesus addresses the distant cousins of the modern day over-churched, under-reached: those who were religious, but not repentant.

> "Not everyone who says to me, 'Lord, Lord,' will enter the
> kingdom of heaven, but only the one who does the will of
> my Father in heaven. On that day many will say to me, 'Lord,
> Lord, didn't we prophesy in your name, drive out demons in
> your name, and do many miracles in your name?' Then I will
> announce to them, 'I never knew you. Depart from me, you
> lawbreakers!'" (Matt. 7:21–23)

Jesus wasn't speaking about atheists, agnostics, pluralists, or
secular humanists. He was directly describing moral and religious
people doing good religious acts in the name of God. These were
the Tom Bradys of religious observance. They had a collection of
lanyards from conferences that would make any worship leader
jealous. Religion was deeply embedded into the routine of their
lives, which gave them full confidence that their acts of righteousness built an impressive résumé setting them up for a big payoff
in heaven.

The old adage that "it isn't *what* you know but *who* you know"
rings true for these religious all-stars and their impressive ac-
complishments. They might have known religion, but they didn't
know the Redeemer standing right in front of them. And therefore "what" they knew didn't really matter all that much. Consider
the petitions Jesus gave as an example in Matthew 7:21–23 in our
modern context. I believe His examples would translate to our era
like this:

Didn't we "say grace" before dinner?
Didn't we vote our values?
Didn't we believe prayer should be allowed in school?
Didn't we go to church?
Didn't we believe in God?

Didn't we get misty eyes whenever we heard "God Bless
   America" sung at a baseball game?
Didn't we give money to the church?
Didn't we treat women with respect?
Didn't we own Bibles?
Didn't we get the baby christened by the priest?
Didn't we want America to return to its Christian roots?
Didn't we stay married and faithful?

The term "self-righteousness" often comes with a connotation of superiority or rigid legalism. And while those might be
results of self-righteousness, the *root* of self-righteousness is the
belief that your own personal works justify you before God. Self-
righteousness believes that you are good enough or can be if you
try hard. Many people function as if they don't need saving, but
that doesn't change the reality that God has given only One mediator and One atonement and that there is no exception clause.

"Didn't We" vs. "Didn't He"

That reality has changed the way I view the mission field. These
petitioners Jesus spoke of loved to say, "didn't we?" when they
should have been saying "didn't He?" They should have put their
trust in a righteousness outside themselves, one that only Jesus
could provide. But there was only one "didn't" that Jesus answered
with, and from His own words, it was that He did not know them.
This may sound strange because Jesus certainly knew them in a
literal sense. The One whom the Scriptures state is "the image of
the invisible God, the firstborn over all creation. For everything
was created by him, in heaven and on earth, the visible and the
invisible" (Col. 1:15–16), certainly knows each person by name.

By not knowing them, He meant He did not know them spiritually because of their sin. By Jesus declaring, "I never knew you," He was claiming that they were not His disciples. They were not in His family and stood as unforgiven "lawbreakers."

They may have known Jewish religion, ritual, and duty, but they didn't know Jesus Christ. They were on a wide road that would lead to their destruction, even though their religious résumés left them assuming they were just fine.

This reality calls us to missional urgency to reach those in our services who are comfortable with Christian lingo but have no understanding of the truth. The message remains: no saving faith exists apart from commitment to Jesus Christ and belief in His gospel. While the number of those who check "No Religion" on a survey might be rising, politicians still invoke vague language about God in their speeches to appease the millions of Americans who get goose bumps singing "God Bless America" at baseball games. This god they are singing of, however, functions more like a national mascot than a God who demands our faith and repentance. The church must awaken to the reality that this is a false gospel with eternal consequences. Cultural Christianity is a mindset that places one's security in heritage, values, rites of passage (such as a first communion or a baptism from childhood), and a generic deity, rather than the redemptive work of Jesus Christ. These false gospels pose serious challenges to pastors and local church members who are seeking to live on mission and remain faithful to the Great Commission where the Lord has them living, working, and being part of local life.

Gospel believers who care about the souls of their friends, coworkers, neighbors, high school teammates, and families need to be knowledgeable about their mission field and understand the task at hand for those of us who live among Cultural Christianity.

Jesus claimed He would tell those religious people to depart from Him because He never knew them. What a statement and what a tragedy! Understanding this mission field has led the church I pastor to clarity and intentionality as we minister to our modern-day Matthew 7:21–23 community. Knowing the cultural religious landscape keeps us focused on gospel-centered efforts to see people move from being "Christians" by culture to Christians by conviction.

We know, from Jesus Himself, that there are people who can be in the church but not of the church. We know there are unsaved "Christians." And we know that Jesus will not be fooled, even if the rest of us pretend to be.

Questions for Discussion and Reflection

- Matthew 7:21–23 informs us that not every religious person will inherit the kingdom of heaven and not every religious person is known by God as an adopted member of His family. What is your gut reaction to that fact?

- If someone asked you why you're a Christian, or more specifically, how you know you're a Christian, what would you say? *Because of what Jesus did & what He is doing with me.*

- Are you tempted to put your faith in anything but the shed blood of Jesus Christ? *No*

- What is your version of "Lord, didn't I _____?" *trust in your work & word*

Religion without Salvation:

Characteristics of Cultural Christianity

Do not flatter yourselves of being good enough, because you are morally so; because you go to church, say the prayers, and take the sacrament, therefore you think no more required; alas, you are deceiving your own souls.
—GEORGE WHITEFIELD

Brad and Sophie Camp are, by most standards, good people. They do things as a family and try to keep their kids involved in various activities. They are considering trading their SUV for a minivan, something Sophie said she would never do. They try their best to have dinner as a family when the kids' schedules permit it, and when the family dinners actually happen, they always hold hands around the dinner table and say "the blessing." When it's her turn to pick the prayer, their four-year-old daughter always picks the "Johnny Appleseed" song: *"Oh the Lord is good to me, and so I thank the Lord for giving me the things I need, the sun and the rain and the apple seed, the Lord is good to me."* She learned this "prayer" at her faith-based preschool where she goes twice a week while Sophie heads to the gym for her yoga class.

On Facebook, a recent family photo on the front steps of a church building has more than one hundred likes and dozens of comments about their beautiful family. The day before, they had gone shopping to get the girls new matching dresses for church. The nine-year-old wasn't thrilled about having to match her baby sister, but Sophie told her she could change clothes as soon as they got home. The Camps are in their midthirties and go to church only about once every three months, because they are just so busy. The extended family on Brad's side has a beach house and they try and get down to it for the weekend whenever the weather is nice. It is also a real hassle to get all the kids out the door on a Sunday morning. (Miraculously, they are able to get everyone ready for school each morning, but nobody has ever brought that up.) When they are in town, they try hard to be at church because it means a lot to Papa and Nana, Sophie's parents.

Papa is a third-generation member of the church and has taught in the same adult "Sunday school" classroom for thirty years. He sings in the choir every now and then but doesn't like some of the new music they've been doing since the church hired the "new guy." Papa serves on several committees at the church and never misses a Sunday. Nana's entire social life revolves around the church, and she is always so thrilled to see the grandkids there so she can show them off to her friends. She and the other ladies teaching children's Sunday school tell the girls that they changed their mom's diaper in the nursery when she was a baby.

Church is a "good thing" in the Camps' eyes, especially for the kids, since it is a place where they learn good moral lessons. And when they finally do make it, they admittedly feel good about themselves—and it gives the kids a chance to wear their mono-grammed "church clothes." Being seen as the family that doesn't take the kids to church would be embarrassing to Nana, and the passive-aggressive comments at family gatherings would be un-bearable. Even when the Camps lived in a different state for Brad's job, Nana would ask Sophie every Monday on the phone whether she "took my grandkids to church." It drove Sophie crazy. Now, being back in the same town, she can't even lie about their church attendance. Attending a different church than Nana and Papa's in the same town would be worse than not attending at all.

Plus the experience is comfortable. During the worship ser-vice, the new minister speaks for twenty minutes about loving others. Jesus is portrayed as a great example of this, since He helped the poor (the church's Habitat for Humanity ministry gets a shameless plug). The pastor doesn't talk about sin, repen-tance, or the blood of Jesus, but gives a very inspiring message, as usual. After church, the Camps always head to Papa and Nana's for lunch, and the kids can't wait to change into their regular clothes. Brad and Sophie have found that they fight less if they occasion-ally give this four-hour sacrifice to Sophie's parents, as it doesn't seem to impact the rest of their normal day-to-day routine.

This is the life of a typical Cultural Christian family.

WHO'S FAKING: A QUICK LOOK AT OTHER TYPES OF UNSAVED CHRISTIANS

Not all "unsaved Christians" are Cultural Christians. While my focus in the book is going to be on cultural and nominal Chris-tianity, I will take a moment to identify other kinds of people who appear to be believers but, according to Scripture, are not. Two primary kinds of unsaved Christians presented in the Bible are:

- **The Wolf in Sheep's Clothing:** Jesus warned His followers to "be on your guard against false prophets who come to you in sheep's clothing but inwardly are ravaging wolves" (Matt. 7:15). Burk Parsons reminds Christians that "false teachers creep into the church not because they look like false teachers but because they look like angels."[1] This is a completely different animal than nominal Christianity. Whereas a Cultural Christian might avoid serious church commitment or think it's unnecessary, the false teacher often digs deep into a community and can pose a serious threat to the church by manipulating and misguiding people. Scripture warns that false teachers:

  - Create division (Rom. 16:17)
  - Deceive with flattery (Rom. 16:18)
  - Appease people by departing from sound doctrine (2 Tim. 4:3)
  - Lead people astray (Matt. 24:11–13)
  - Take people captive through bad philosophy and theology (Col. 2:8)
  - Seem to have spiritual power and authority to deceive even the elect (Matt. 24:24)
  - Are bringing upon themselves a swift destruction (2 Peter 2:1)

- **The Hypocrite:** This is a person who wears the mask of a Christian in order to be seen and admired by others, with no desire to actually follow or worship Christ (Matt.

6:5–6). This person is exclusively external, and only concerned with having the "veneer of public virtue to cover the rot of private vice."[2] John Blanchard calls hypocrisy "nothing better than skin deep holiness."[3] While the false prophet might be seeking to deceive others to a false gospel, the hypocrite seeks to deceive others for their own pride or appearance. Like the Pharisees of Jesus' day, these people often have a skewed, elitist view of their own morality, yet are unmistakably missing the fruit of a heart changed by God. This kind of unsaved Christianity is perhaps more individualistic, but this, too, is different from nominal Christianity, as the hypocrite is likely aware of his own moral dissonance.

Entire books could be written on each of these unsaved "Christians," but it is important to specify that these are not the groups I will be discussing in this book. Cultural Christians are those who genuinely believe they are on good terms with God because of church familiarity, a generic moral code, political affiliation, a religious family heritage, etc. Cultural Christianity is largely based on *confusion*, whereas the hypocrite and the false teacher have a "Christianity" based on *deceit*.

Middle School Awakening

My exposure to Cultural Christianity began primarily with my own upbringing. I grew up going to church every Sunday, unless I was sick or out of town. Our family would say a memorized prayer before eating together at the dining room table each night: "God is great, God is good, let us thank Him for our food." This type of prayer is a nightly tradition for many Cultural Christian families with young children. I owned a Bible, which was given to me after my confirmation at the neighborhood Methodist church, but I don't remember reading it. I knew about Noah and the Ark, David and Goliath, and that Jesus helped a lot of people.

In middle school, a pretty girl invited me to a Fellowship of Christian Athletes (FCA) "huddle meeting." I played sports and believed in God, and did I mention she was pretty? So I went. FCA was a great time, and I went every week to the huddle meeting with other classmates. We would hear something the kids called a "testimony" from athletes who played football for the Florida State Seminoles, and I thought it was the coolest.

As the school year went on, it was time for our fall retreat. I had never heard of one of those things. It was a one-day event in a camp-type setting held about an hour from where I lived. The thought of getting on a bus and spending the day with my friends and playing in sports competitions sounded like my type of thing, and I signed up as quickly as my parents agreed to let me go. After dodgeball, kickball, and some relay races, we had our assembly time. The speaker was a large man who had played professional football, and I remember thinking his muscles were bigger than Hulk Hogan's. He told really funny stories and then starting talking about our need to trust in Jesus, that He died for our sins and rose from the grave.

Up until this FCA retreat, if anyone had asked me if I was a Christian, I would have said yes without hesitation. But if you had asked me why I claimed to be a Christian (nobody ever had), trusting in Jesus and that He died for me would not have been my answer. And as for sins? I didn't really have a concept of my sinfulness. I got in trouble every now and then, but I figured the real bad guys were people who were in jail and the Russian tag team I would watch each Saturday in pro wrestling.

The speaker gave what I now know is called an "invitation" to respond to his presentation of the gospel. At the time, I had never been to an event where the speaker had asked anyone to "come forward" and trust in Jesus Christ. He counted to three and asked people to come forward who wanted to be saved from their sins by "giving their lives to Jesus Christ." The preacher talked about the blood of Jesus and heaven and hell. He told the packed basket-ball gymnasium of middle school students that we needed to ask God to forgive us for sinning against Him, we needed to repent of our sins, and become followers of Jesus.

Dozens of students stood up and walked forward to meet with FCA staff members to give their lives to Jesus. I didn't move, because as far as I was concerned, I was a Christian. Sin, Jesus' blood, and my need for repentance were new things to my ears, but I was fairly certain I was okay. My reasoning was simple: I believed in God, I wasn't of any other religion (like Judaism or Islam), I went to church on Sundays, and I was in FCA. I had never thought about trusting in Jesus because nobody had ever told me I needed to do so, but I figured since I went to church already, I was fine and probably had already done all those things.

Then something happened that opened my eyes, truly freaked me out, and changed my life. The speaker said, "There is one more thing I want to share for some of you still in your seats." He then read the words of Jesus from Matthew 7:21–23.

"Not everyone who says to me, 'Lord, Lord,' will enter the kingdom of heaven, but only the one who does the will of my Father in heaven. On that day many will say to me, 'Lord, Lord, didn't we prophesy in your name, drive out demons in

your name, and do many miracles in your name?' Then I will
announce to them, 'I never knew you. Depart from me, you
lawbreakers!'" (Matt. 7:21–23)

I don't remember his commentary exactly, but he shouted that
there were people in the room who went to church, came from good
families, said a prayer before meals, but had never trusted in Jesus
Christ. "You are no more a Christian than someone who doesn't
believe in God at all, and that will lead you straight to hell! God will
not let sin go unpunished. You need forgiveness for your sins, and
only Jesus can give you that forgiveness because He took on the
punishment that you deserved, even though He had never sinned."

I know that's not always the best way to share the gospel, but
it certainly got through to me. He gave a second invitation, and
I believed he was speaking directly to me. I walked down to the
front completely freaked out. I had thought hell was for really bad
people who committed crimes like murder, not for someone like
me. It is where evil dictators went, not middle-schoolers from nice
families who went to church and had a picture in the Olan Mills
church directory to prove it. This muscular, enthusiastic preacher
was talking about a Jesus with
whom I was unfamiliar. "The
gospel" in my mind was a kind of
music where people wore choir
robes and clapped. I had no idea
it was about Jesus dying on the
cross for me, or that His death
even mattered. I walked for-
ward, prayed to trust in Christ with a staff member named Walter,
and I was angry. Don't get me wrong, I experienced joy over this
great news about my sins being forgiven, but I was upset. How

> **How was it that I had been to church my entire life and nobody had ever told me this news?**

was it that I had been to church my entire life and nobody had ever told me this news?

Getting Uncomfortable

My story is far from unique. We can trace its roots back to Matthew 7:21–23, and unfortunately, that "family tree" is still spreading today. Being a self-identified Christian for cultural reasons, rather than the good news of the gospel, is commonplace in America.

> **Being a self-identified Christian for cultural reasons, rather than the good news of the gospel, is commonplace in America.**

This widespread complacency and ignorance should call the church to action.

Let's circle back to the fictitious Camp family.

If asked about their faith, they wouldn't be uncomfortable, but would respond with answers about going to church and being good people. Church is a place where basic social expectations are met in the name of morals, family, and tradition. This is understandable, since the idea of church isn't linked much to belief in Jesus or any demand the Scriptures would place on those who claim to be Christians. It is very important to the Camps that they be viewed as good people, the way they portray themselves on social media. They want to be seen as a well-rounded American family that goes to church when they can. The Camps are not defensive or awkward when it comes to questions about their beliefs. They certainly believe in God and, as far as they are concerned, they always have and always will.

But if the conversation moved to questions about Jesus, salvation, and the gospel, it would be a different story. They might nod and smile, but suddenly they'd feel awkward because they would be clueless about what any of those questions about Jesus and the gospel have to do with them personally. They already see themselves as Christians. "Salvation" is something only the crazy guy on the street corner talks about. It is for the extreme people, the weird religious types.

One might assume that the most tragic component of the Camps' story is their cluelessness about the gospel. But there is something deeper to their sudden awkwardness in a theological conversation that makes it very difficult to present the gospel: the tragic reality that the Camps don't believe they actually need Jesus. They have had plenty of exposure to Christian lingo, they were at church as recently as Easter Sunday, they know about Jesus, and their "faith is important" to them. This beautiful, loving, moral, American family is "Christian" without Christ.

When we think of unreached people groups, we envision intrepid missionaries taking the gospel to a place where the name of Jesus has never been spoken. But many American pastors are faced with a similarly daunting task: to bring Jesus to a place where He is admired but not worshiped, where God is a grandpa in the sky, where many of their congregants are "good people" who don't know they need to be saved. Like their New Testament counterparts from Matthew 7, they know religion, but don't realize that their religion is the very thing from which they need to be saved. I try to imagine the faces of those calling "Lord, Lord" when Jesus told them that they wouldn't be going to heaven. Their religious résumés were something to admire, yet Jesus wasn't impressed—He was outraged. Rather than calling them good people, He called them "lawbreakers."

To modern-day Cultural Christians, just like the religious people in Matthew 7, the idea of being "saved" is unnecessary.

After all, they're good people who live moral lives. Cultural Christians have faith and they don't consider themselves atheists, but their god is a generic deity rather than the God of the Bible. My friend Matt back in the seminary parking lot would have called them "over-churched and under-reached." They could also be called "almost-Christians." But sadly, an almost-Christian is as outright lost as an atheist who wouldn't go to church on his best day, even if Nana insisted. Like the fictional Camp family, and like I did at thirteen at the FCA retreat, these people need Jesus. But they are so difficult to reach because they believe they already have Him. He is just a Jesus without a gospel, and that is no Jesus at all.

Questions for Discussion and Reflection

- What is the spiritual temperature of your own heart? High Your own household? High Your local church? High Your community? Low

- Do you live in a place where Jesus is admired but not worshiped? Yes

3

Civic Religion:

Generic Faith That Demands and Asks Nothing of Its Followers

You have made us for yourself,
and our heart is restless until it rests in you.
—AUGUSTINE

Every person in the city of Cincinnati is a Christian.

That's at least how it felt when I went to the Great American Ballpark to see the Reds play on a hot summer afternoon. The stadium was full of fans who had shown up to watch the Reds take on the Chicago Cubs. There was a loud applause after the national anthem was sung, and a fifth-inning home run brought the hometown fans to their feet as the Reds took the lead against their division rivals. But the cheers after that towering home run to center field were nothing compared to the crowd's reaction in the middle of the seventh-inning.

One of my favorite parts of any Major League Baseball game is called the "seventh-inning stretch." This is where the fans from

both teams stand up and stretch their arms and legs while singing the classic song, "Take Me Out to the Ball Game." It is a great
tradition that brings families and friends together to sing loudly,
without a care in the world. For just a moment, all fans are supporting the same thing—the great game of baseball. Legend
claims the song first played at a ballpark at a high school in Los
Angeles in 1934. The song became synonymous with the seventh-
inning stretch when broadcaster Harry Caray would lead the fans
in singing the song during Chicago White Sox games (and later in
his career, with the crosstown rival, Chicago Cubs).

But this particular day at the Reds game, the seventh-inning
stretch did not deliver quite the nostalgia I was hoping for. This
happened to be a Sunday, and ever since the terror attacks on the
United States on September 11, 2001, Major League ballparks
have a new seventh-inning tradition. On Sundays, singing about
peanuts and crackerjacks gets set aside for a more somber display.
During the middle of the seventh-inning on any Sunday game,
every Major League ballpark pauses, brings out the players from
each team to stand in a line with their hats removed, and plays the
song "God Bless America" for all to sing. (The New York Yankees
practice this tradition at each home game, but the other Major
League teams observe this as a Sunday tradition.) This Sunday in
Cincinnati, 45,000 people stood and sang at the top of their lungs,
asking God to bless America.

I've been to Christian conferences that filled arenas and
nobody sang about God this loudly and cheered so passionately
at the conclusion. I stood there and wondered if the ovation after
the final note was louder than when the Reds upset the Oakland
A's by sweeping them in the 1990 World Series. As soon as the
song was over, we went into "Take Me Out to the Ball Game," and

I felt my favorite part of being a fan had the thunder stolen in the name of God blessing our nation.

The Mission Field in Our Backyard

After the game, I had plans to meet up with some local church planters from my denomination, as is customary for me when I travel. I find that connecting with other church planters is always inspiring, and it is probably nice for them to have someone treat them to a meal or dessert, as church planting can be very difficult. These particular church planters came to Cincinnati because the North American Mission Board (NAMB) had identified it as a "Send City." NAMB's church planting strategy emphasizes highly populated areas with a low number of evangelical churches per capita. Knowing this, I had been so caught off guard by the crowd's enthusiasm during the seventh-inning festivities, I actually paused during the game to "research" NAMB's evaluation of Cincinnati. Apparently, I thought, there wasn't a need for church planting in this city because nothing got the crowd more excited than singing about God and asking Him to bless America. To my surprise, the "Send Cincinnati" information revealed that just 13.7 percent of metro Cincinnati residents were affiliated with an evangelical church.[1] *13.7 percent.* That rate is bad even when we're talking tips at a cheap diner. But as a percentage of people affiliated with a local evangelical church? No wonder NAMB had identified this as a mission field.

So, then, who were all of these people singing so loudly?

That day in Ohio, I was reminded that Cultural Christianity isn't just an epidemic of the American South. I had just witnessed thousands of people worshiping enthusiastically in the church of civic religion.

Civic religion is practiced from the high school football locker room, where teams incorporate a prayer before the game, to the grand stages of Hollywood, where you can find a celebrity thanking God during an acceptance speech. It is rampant in American politics and is expected from national leaders, though the reasoning for that falls somewhere between tradition and sentimentality. Of course there are those who go bananas over "God language" in the name of separation of church and state, but that hasn't yet been able to kill the American practice of sprinkling in sentimental religious language when needed. Has a modern-day sitting president of the United States ever failed to say "God Bless America" as the closing in a major address to the nation? While it is certainly a nice gesture (and I'm sure some have had sincere Christian faith), these small nods to God keep civic religion and Cultural Christianity alive.

Civic religion promotes a god without any definition and a generic faith that demands and asks nothing of its followers. Participants stretch across the cultural spectrum in terms of geography and socioeconomic status. In some areas, civic religion is even proudly theistic and likes the idea of Jesus. Selective words spoken by Jesus in the New Testament will be used and cited when the political cause of the day needs a rally cry. Whether it is government-run healthcare, the death penalty, same-sex marriage, or immigration, Jesus is positioned as having an opinion that can suit one's side, regardless of one's adherence to the authority of Scripture as a whole.

Moralistic Therapeutic Deism

This civic religion also plays into the daily lives of individuals, creating a type of "moral deism." This phrase is derived from

"Moralistic Therapeutic Deism," a concept coined and explained by sociologists Christian Smith and Melinda Lundquist Denton in their book, *Soul Searching: The Religious and Spiritual Lives of American Teenagers*. Al Mohler identifies this as the "new American religion,"[2] and its tenets can be summarized as follows:

1. "A God exists who created and orders the world and watches over human life on earth."
2. "God wants people to be good, nice, and fair to each other, as taught in the Bible and by most world religions."
3. "The central goal of life is to be happy and to feel good about oneself."
4. "God does not need to be particularly involved in one's life except when God is needed to resolve a problem."
5. "Good people go to heaven when they die."[3]

Despite the fact that these principles align closely with the beliefs of many Americans, most people have never self-identified as "moral deists"—they just call themselves "Christians." When asked to indicate their religion on an application or form, many Americans, without hesitation, would check "Christian." By this, they mean to say that they are "good people" who believe in God but aren't Jewish or Muslim. But the word "Christian" in itself implies Christ, and notice that He is missing entirely from the description of this "new American religion" of moral deism.

Many people who are comfortable with the idea of God and familiar with some image of Jesus have no concept of what the gospel of Christ actually is. There is a perception amongst Cultural Christians that the gospel is for more extreme, perhaps "born again" people. Mainstream Cultural Christians aren't wrapped up in promoting some kind of gospel message. They are simply trying to be nice to others, pursue their idea of personal happiness, pray when something bad happens, and rest in the belief that they are going to heaven after they die.

Jesus-Admiring vs. Jesus-Following

But I want to take a moment to address a different kind of person—perhaps someone who would say they love Jesus, someone who has a greater familiarity with the Bible, and is maybe even deeply involved in local church life. At the surface, these people may not be easily distinguishable from true believers—which is why reaching them with the truth of Scripture is so crucial. I'll call them *Jesus-Admiring* moral deists. Like Peter in Matthew 16, they can confess that Jesus is Messiah but don't ascribe to that the implication of death (with Christ, and consequently, to one's self). Peter didn't have a category in his mind for a Messiah who dies before the end of the story. He was looking for a victorious savior to alleviate political, economic, and social injustices, not someone who would be killed off just as He was gaining fame. In twenty-first century America, we have no excuse—we have a completed Bible and we know the end of the story. But how often are we looking for a king who exemplifies and grants earthly decorations of success? In the Jesus of the Bible, though, we find instead a call to die.

Self-proclaimed Christians who worship a god that requires no self-sacrifice, no obedience, no submission, and no surrender are not worshiping the God of the Bible, no matter how much they claim they love Jesus. In His own words, Jesus tells us what it looks like to love Him: "If you love me, you will keep my commands" (John 14:15); "If anyone loves me, he will keep my word" (John 14:23). Many people want the good-luck-charm Jesus, not the sacrificial Lamb of God whose death requires action.

As a kid, I heard an illustration that has stuck with me over the years. A speaker had us measure the distance between our heads and our literal hearts—the left side of our heads to the middle of the left side of our chests. For most people it's about eighteen inches. As we wrapped up, the speaker said, "Some of you are going to miss heaven by eighteen inches."

> **Self-proclaimed Christians who worship a god that requires no self-sacrifice, no obedience, no submission, and no surrender are not worshiping the God of the Bible, no matter how much they claim they love Jesus.**

Scripture tells us that an intellectual grasp of the gospel story (even the *whole* gospel story) is not enough to save: "You believe that God is one. Good! Even the demons believe—and they shudder" (James 2:19). Belief in God without the Christ of the cross is a deficient faith—even demons have that! But a life transformed by true gospel understanding will result in a heart of worship and a desire to follow God. Knowledge alone does not equate to saving faith.

Looking back at the Reds game in Cincinnati, I'm tempted to ask whether or not the god we sang to was the same god the politician asks to bless America at the closing of a speech, and the same god the winning quarterback thanks during the post-game interview. I'm curious about the answer, but recognize this is not the most important question. The issue of importance is whether this god is the God of Abraham, Isaac, and Jacob. Is this god "Yahweh," the God of Israel, who "in these last days . . . has spoken to us by his Son," Jesus Christ (Heb. 1:2)? It is hard to know the answer, but it matters for the church on mission, because a faith clothed in Christian language that doesn't find its definition in the person and work of Jesus Christ is not a Christian faith. Jesus dismisses it altogether (Matt. 7:21–23). I wonder why we often don't do the same.

Theologian A. W. Tozer wrote that the most important thing about someone is what comes to mind when they think about God.[4] For the Cultural Christian practicing civic religion, it is usually morality and a sense of national pride clothed in Judeo-Christian language. I wonder how many people at that Reds game fall into the 13.7 percent of Cincinnatians in local evangelical churches. I wonder what they really think about the God in the song we sang. While I know we serve a merciful God, I can't help but return again to the dismissive words of Jesus in Matthew 7:

> "Not everyone who says to me, 'Lord, Lord,' will enter the kingdom of heaven, but only the one who does the will of my Father in heaven. On that day many will say to me, 'Lord, Lord, didn't we prophesy in your name, drive out demons in your name, and do many miracles in your name?' Then I will announce to them, 'I never knew you. Depart from me, you lawbreakers!'"

If Jesus walked into that stadium in Cincinnati on that Sunday for the seventh-inning stretch, would He say, "Many will say to me, 'Didn't I sing "God Bless America" at the Reds game and get goose bumps?'" While there is certainly nothing wrong with singing patriotic songs that include a reference to God, where is the disconnect between mere theistic belief, moral deism, or an admiration of Jesus, and actually believing the gospel and following Him?

Questions for
Discussion and Reflection

- The god of moral deism requires nothing and expects nothing of his followers. He blesses but does not discipline, tips his hat of favor but does not rebuke. Is this similar to your understanding of God? *NO*

- Can you think of any friends or loved ones who understand God in this manner? In what ways can you share with them that the true God is better than this caricature? *Yes*

*God expects us to live for Him
We can expect Him to disciple us when
we don't obey Him*

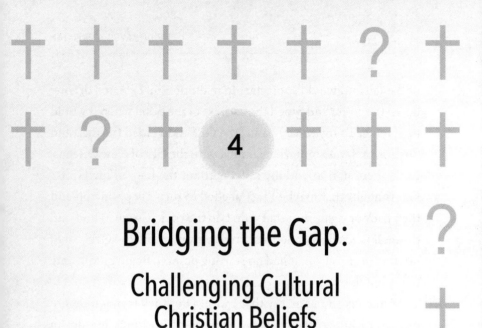

Bridging the Gap:
Challenging Cultural Christian Beliefs

> The antithesis between the Christian life and the life of bourgeois respectability is at an end. The Christian life comes to mean nothing more than living in the world and as the world, in being no different from the world, in fact, in being prohibited from being different from the world for the sake of grace. The upshot of it all is that my only duty as a Christian is to leave the world for an hour or so on a Sunday morning and go to church to be assured that my sins are all forgiven. I need no longer try to follow Christ, for cheap grace, the bitterest foe of discipleship, which true discipleship must loathe and detest, has freed me from that.
>
> —DIETRICH BONHOEFFER

Few things get me more flustered than trying to find my way around a big city. Just one wrong turn can become a twenty-minute detour to get back on the correct route. Once, on a visit to New Orleans, I dropped my phone in the parking lot while leaving a restaurant. At first, I thought there was minimal damage. Little did I know that the GPS in my phone was broken as a result of the fall and would soon start to malfunction. I started driving down the street and typed the address of the hotel where I would be staying. To my (near) panic, the GPS didn't load the map and directions. I was somewhat familiar with the city of New Orleans, but not enough to find my hotel without the help of my GPS. I first thought that maybe I just needed to turn my phone off and then back on again, but that didn't do the trick. Come to find out, the *destination* had loaded just fine on my map, but the GPS could not find *my* location. It had no starting point to begin guiding me to my hotel.

After a rush of anxiety that I would be stuck trying to figure out who I knew in New Orleans to come and pick me up on the side of the road, I decided to go "old school" by calling the hotel and having them give me step-by-step directions. "I'll just give you the address and you could enter it into your phone," the lady insisted. "Ma'am, I'm not in an emotional state to have this conversation, just please give me directions." After closely and nervously following the directions given to me over the phone, I arrived at the hotel, having indigestion that could not be blamed on my Cajun dinner.

> **The hallmark of Cultural Christianity is typically familiarity (or even comfort) with biblical principles without a sense of personal need for salvation.**

My experience in New Orleans gave me a crash course on the importance of a "starting point." A vague general direction is not the same as a direct path from one discrete point to another. Similarly, the biggest obstacle that a believer might face in evangelism to Cultural Christians is the difficulty in finding one's spiritual location or an actual starting point. I've heard this described as "theological triage." *What does this person believe? What does this person know about Jesus? The cross? The Bible?* This is certainly a generalization, but the hallmark of Cultural Christianity is typically familiarity (or even comfort) with biblical principles without a sense of personal need for salvation. But even this is a wide net, and there's no clear way to come at someone and debunk the falsehoods they've believed without first digging through what they do believe.

Compare that to a spiritual conversation focused on evangelism with an atheist. While atheists' stories, circumstances, or reasons for their personal conclusions about the existence of God vary, there is a clear starting point for a conversation, and that is unbelief. Conversations with Jews, Muslims, Buddhists, Mormons, and Hindus also have a starting point. When speaking with a follower of a different religion, Christians can begin conversations with what those religions believe compared to what the Bible teaches. Cultural Christians claim to admire the Bible and are not atheists, Muslims, or Hindus. They attend a church service on Easter Sunday and have songs about the historic birth of Christ playing in their homes at Christmastime. These factors make a starting point for an evangelistic conversation unclear and complicated.

Finding Common Ground

Starting points are important for any intentional spiritual conversation. An understanding of where to begin is essential for a purposeful dialogue about where one stands with God. Cultural Christians (like many Americans) believe they are good people. Those who perceive they are good people might need Jesus to take the wheel on a bad day, but not necessarily to forgive the sins they don't think they have actually committed. In this religion of

Cultural Christianity, good people make occasional mistakes, but sinning is for the really bad people, who are probably in prison. Atheists don't think they need God because they don't believe God exists. The Cultural Christian would be offended to be thought of as someone who needs the gospel, yet only believes they need God when they need people to pray before a surgery or job interview. Many Cultural Christians believe Jesus died on the cross, but in a generic sense rather than as a substitute for the sins of the individual.

Starting a gospel conversation with a Cultural Christian friend can be frustrating. Discovering a starting point will not make a conversation more comfortable, but it will allow clarity to develop concerning differences between a cultural religion and the actual Christian faith. At the outset, Cultural Christians usually believe the only difference between you and them is that you are just a little more "into" Christianity and perhaps extreme.

So where is one to begin in conversation?

Start with the God of the Bible

As my friend Matt explained in the seminary parking lot, Cultural Christians have to see themselves as lost before they can actually see their need to be saved. This is the most foundational missional truth of reaching Cultural Christians. It's also the most challenging.

This process of "getting someone lost" has a starting point, and that starting point is God Himself. It has been said that the most important question one can ask is not "Is there a God?" (this is especially helpful to remember, because for the Cultural Christian that is not a question up for debate), but rather, "If there is a God, has he spoken?" Likewise, Tozer claimed that the most important thing about a person is what comes to their mind when they think about God.[1] Perhaps Tozer knew that our very thoughts about God would form our thinking about our need for God. The good news for all is that God has not left us to wonder who He is or what He has said. Rather, He has revealed Himself to humanity through His written Word, where those thoughts should be rooted and answers found.

While Cultural Christians may not truly believe every part of the Bible, they likely won't scoff if you use it as the foundation for a spiritual conversation. I have rarely met a Cultural Christian who did not have some level of respect for the Bible. In fact, when confronted with the truth of the Bible, I've known some Cultural Christians to quickly acknowledge the disconnect between what Scripture says and what they've believed. One friend in particular came to Christ because he couldn't help but dwell on this disconnect.

Many people get defensive when personal character is questioned, but in terms of navigating common ground for an evangelistic discussion, most Cultural Christians will not reject God's Word outright. While the Bible might get you mocked by an atheist, Cultural Christians claim a respect and even belief in the Bible. They will certainly have one somewhere in their home (and perhaps a Bible app on their phone).

The God of the Bible Is Holy

In that Bible, at the very beginning, God presents Himself as holy. After the first human sin in history, Adam and Eve hid (Gen. 3:8). They were not playing a fun game of hide-and-seek with their Creator. They were aware of something even greater than their sin. They were aware of who their sin was against.

A belief in God's holiness should lead to a realization that God should be feared. Outside of the Bible, this is nearly impossible in Cultural Christianity because a generic god is not defined.

Sinning against a "big man upstairs" leaves one with no reason to hide when they sin. This god functions as a Mother Nature figure, a distant force. J. I. Packer wrote, "Unless we see our shortcomings in the light of the law and holiness of God, we do not see them *as sin* at all."[2] This god is far from the one whom the seraphim declared "holy, holy, holy" to the prophet Isaiah (Isa. 6:3). A high view of the holiness of God gives us self-awareness about our standing before God. Isaiah responded to the revelation given to him about God by declaring himself to be "a man of unclean lips" (6:5).

God's Holiness Means Sin Is Serious

In the book of Romans, we get the most complete description of the saving work of Jesus Christ in the entire Bible. Romans spells out the implications of Christ's work for the life of the believer and unpacks paramount doctrines of the Christian faith such as justification and sanctification. Before Paul gets to informing the reader of the riches of our call to salvation, justification, sanctification, and Christian living, he has a clear starting point for understanding why these doctrines even matter. The reason salvation is needed is because God is holy, and He will not let sin go unpunished.

Paul sets the stage, explaining God's holiness and our failure to acknowledge Him. "They exchanged the truth of God for a lie, and worshiped and served what has been created instead of the Creator, who is praised forever" (Rom. 1:25). Rather than worshiping our Creator, we chose to worship what was created. Because of this willful rebellion against God, all offenders "deserve to die" (Rom. 1:32).

If God Is Holy, What Are We?

Paul continues with his starting point by informing the reader that because of your hardened and unrepentant heart you are storing up wrath for yourself in the day of wrath, when God's righteous judgment is revealed. He will repay each one according to his works: eternal life to those who by persistence in doing good seek glory, honor, and immortality; but wrath and anger to those who are self-seeking and disobey the truth while obeying unrighteousness. (Rom. 2:5–8)

Paul then identifies the spiritual location of humanity apart from Jesus Christ by quoting the psalmist:

There is no one righteous, not even one.
There is no one who understands;
there is no one who seeks God.
All have turned away;
all alike have become worthless.
There is no one who does what is good,
not even one. (Rom. 3:10–12)

The reality is that people are not sinners because they sin. They sin because they are sinners. We all inherit a sinful nature from our first parent, Adam, and then prove we are his offspring by sinning ourselves.

As a middle school student just starting my teenage years, I would have never considered myself a sinner. Did I occasionally do something wrong that would cause my parents to send me to my room all night? Yes, but what's the big deal? I served my punishment by missing out on the movie or whatever my friends were doing. I would have my privileges back in the morning. "Sinning" was something reserved for really bad people like the ones I learned about in my mainline Protestant Sunday school. Goliath,

Nebuchadnezzar, and Jonah (before the fish swallowed him)—
those were the bad guys. I wasn't a sinner, because I went to church,
prayed before dinner, and did more good deeds than bad. I was also
an Inserra, and we are good people, after all. If the most important
thing about me was what came to my mind when I thought about
God, I wasn't worshiping the God of the Bible. I was giving occasional nods to a superhero character who beat the bad guys in the
Old Testament but was also kind of like Santa, who would answer
my bedtime prayers if I stayed off the naughty list. Falling on the
right side of the list usually meant not being *that* bad, like the bully
at school or the kid that always got put in time-out during recess
time on the playground.

For the Cultural Christian, morality is usually determined
by how you're perceived by others. It can also be influenced by
whether you're somewhat identified with a church or by how
well you provide for your family.
A belief in the holiness of God
should expose this thinking as
ridiculous as believing ordering a
Diet Coke cancels out the cheese-
burgers and fries at a fast-food
restaurant. All the good deeds per-
formed tomorrow won't cancel
out the sin that was done today.
Nor do the good deeds done several years ago. Only a high view
of God's holiness can make that understanding possible. When
God is understood as holy, sin cannot go unpunished. There are
no mulligans, participation trophies, or awards for a good effort.

> **For the Cultural Christian, morality is usually determined by how you're perceived by others.**

Good People Go to Heaven?

The most common belief in Cultural Christianity is that good people go to heaven. They believe heaven is a real place. The problem is that this heaven has everything to do with an eternal vacation to Hawaii in the clouds and little to do with God Himself. In the minds of many, being a good person is merely an issue of comparison. Just keep up with those you see as good and disassociate with people with bad reputations. When other people are the standard of goodness, you can always find people a little worse than yourself.

But when God is the standard and I compare myself to Him, the only response can be, "God, have mercy on me, a sinner!" (Luke 18:13). That plea doesn't exist without recognizing the holiness of God. When we finally realize we are great sinners, we can finally understand that we have a great Savior.

The love of God is something a Cultural Christian sentimentally affirms. But the idea of a loving God means little if that God isn't a holy God who so loved the world that He gave His Son to be our substitute and die a death that we deserved. If we desire for our friends and family to understand the love of God, they must come to an understanding that they don't deserve to be loved. "While we were still sinners, Christ died for us" (Rom. 5:8 ESV). This is how the love of God is known (Rom. 5:8).

Conversing with Cultural Christians

Here are some tips to remember when establishing a starting point in a spiritual conversation with a Cultural Christian.

- **Many Cultural Christians claim to revere the Bible.** So feel free to refer to it as the authority on all things sooner than you might if talking to someone of another faith. You have a wide open door to use the Bible as your point of reasoning with people who already claim to believe it is a sacred text. Many of them have church affiliations that don't use the Bible much, so it is likely that they have no idea what the Bible they claim to believe in actually says.

- **Lovingly ask frustrating questions.** "What is the standard for good?" "How good is good enough?" "How many more good deeds do you need to have than bad?" "Who actually doesn't make it to heaven?" Ask these questions to uncover their source of authority for their stated beliefs. The reality is that most Cultural Christians won't be able to answer these questions. The point of this is not to mock them or embarrass them with "gotcha" questions. It's to establish a starting point of what God has told us about Himself, our sin, and the solution found in Jesus Christ.

- **Ask about the Ten Commandments.** There's a good chance they can name some of them. Ask them how they've done in keeping them and if there is any consequence for breaking them. If not, why did God give them to us?

- **Cultural Christians claim a belief in Jesus Christ.** They also believe He died on the cross. If good people go to heaven, why did Jesus die? Is anything more confusing than a Savior dying for people who really didn't need saving?

Many people I have baptized were former Cultural Christians who could not answer these types of questions. In their frustration, they began to realize something really was dissonant. The Christian faith they claimed to have held had little to do with anything the Bible said, outside of trying to be a good neighbor. Once their eyes were opened to the reality of God's holiness and their personal sin, a need for a Savior was understood. A starting point was established and a need for the gospel believed.

For example, I have a friend who is your salt-of-the-earth coach and has served as a father figure to dozens and dozens of kids in town. He has had great impact on young men for several decades. In terms of "religion," he didn't have a connection to a local church but would watch well-known televangelists on TV from time to time. But then, he heard the gospel. The message of God's holiness, our rebellion, our need for salvation, Jesus' fulfillment of the requirements of the law in our place, and the eternal security that we find in Jesus alone woke him up to the reality that belief in this gospel changes everything in our lives. He realized that (1) his well-intentioned good deeds didn't change the fact that he was a sinner and needed forgiveness, and (2) that what he had heard at a gospel-preaching church was way different from encouraging self-help with biblical themes and a Jesus mascot.

Christians may be intimidated to start gospel conversations out of fear of not knowing the answers to every question or being ready to field every objection. But you may find that simply stating the gospel basics can be enough to turn on a light bulb in someone's mind.

Remember that we're looking for a starting point, not a one-stop-shop to full gospel understanding. Don't enter these conversations as debates, but rather feel confident in simply expressing what the gospel is. Pray that God would provide the wisdom you need to then walk someone through their resulting questions. My friend's realization that he needed Jesus led eventually to saving faith, baptism, deep commitment to a local church, and spiritual growth. But that first began with a starting point—hearing the gospel and understanding it was news.

Questions for
Discussion and Reflection

- The gospel is news! Not advice. Not self-help. We also know that God alone changes hearts. Does this make evangelism seem less intimidating? *Yes*

- Have you ever tried to have a spiritual conversation with a nominal Christian friend or loved one? *Yes* Was it evident to both of you that there was dissonance? *Yes*

- How can you approach that gap next as an evangelistic opportunity? *Yes*

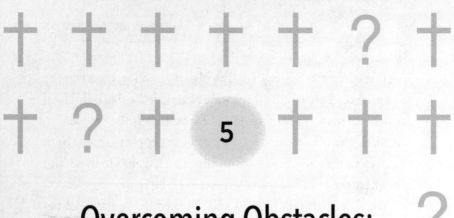

Overcoming Obstacles:

Barriers to Reaching Cultural Christians

Thou mayest enjoy sermons, sacraments,
Sabbaths, seasons of grace, the society of
saints, and yet miss at last of salvation.
—GEORGE SWINNOCK

"How do you get people who loved your sermon to understand that you were actually talking about them?" My friend and church member asked me this question after he had some of his friends join him on a Sunday morning. We regularly emphasize to the congregation the need to invite friends to church. We believe it is a crucial part of being on mission for Christ. My friend was especially happy to have these friends coming to church because he knew what they didn't: they were Cultural Christians and he was hoping that they would notice the difference in how they understood being a Christian and what the Bible says about being a Christian.

This particular Sunday, I had an object-lesson sermon where I used props as a visual aid. There were chairs on the stage, and I described different types of people and what beliefs they represent. The main idea of the visual was to challenge people to think about which chair they are actually sitting in when it comes to their faith and where they need to move if it is the wrong chair.

The first chair represented what I called the "convinced believer." This person is certainly not perfect, but believes the gospel of Jesus Christ and responds to that gospel by repenting of sin and striving to follow Christ. The first-chair person has Christian conviction, drawn from the Bible, that daily impacts his life. The first-chair person is one who has trusted in Jesus Christ for his salvation and repented of his sins.

The second chair represented an unbeliever. This could be an atheist, an agnostic, someone of a different belief system, or just someone who is indifferent about matters of faith. This person is not a Christian (and would admit that).

The third chair is where I spent a great deal of the sermon. That chair was represented by what I called the "falsely assured believer," the unsaved Christian. I included "believer" in the title because an unsaved Christian has grown up in a culture where one can be a "Christian" without Jesus.

Common Cultural Christian Barriers

After the service, my friend told me that all his friends who were at church that morning were in the third chair, but even after listening to my sermon describe what that looks like, they still didn't realize it. I informed him that there are huge barriers that have been built for decades (even generations) that keep his friends from realizing the "chair" where they sit. These barriers have created a lifelong misunderstanding of what it means to be a Christian, and they can be difficult to topple. Here are five primary barriers.

Belief

Cultural Christians believe in God and they believe in heaven. It might seem like a strange paradox that belief in God is actually a barrier to reaching someone for Christ. Cultural Christians are not atheists. To suggest otherwise would be viewed as quite offensive, since believing in God is a given for them. This theism extends well beyond the mere belief that there is a God, higher power, big man in the sky, or something out there. Cultural Christians believe that Jesus was born in Bethlehem and that His mom's name was Mary. They may even have words like "faith" and "hope" in their home décor. Just below the belief-inspired signs is where the nativity scene is set up for the month of December. They can also tell you exactly what is celebrated on Easter Sunday. Knowing stories of the Bible and believing they actually happened are commonplace in Cultural Christianity.

In his New Testament letter, James had something passionate and pointed to say about basic belief: "You believe that God is one. Good! Even the demons believe—and they shudder" (James 2:19). James was not impressed with a knowledge of Christian facts alone. The "faith" of James's audience was deficient, lacking a response to the gospel that would compel them to accompany their beliefs with good works. James compared this faith to the faith of demons. I often wonder when I read that passage if James sounded extreme by making such a comparison. He was unimpressed by a belief system that didn't result in actually living for Christ, and he called that faith "dead." Holding to some basic beliefs was not going to do the trick in the kingdom of God. It is difficult to point people to their need to trust in Christ when they

Believing in God does not make one a Christian.

already believe the basic facts about Him. James wasn't afraid to "go there" by claiming that even the demons believe those things. He was addressing specific issues for professing—yet falsely assured—believers. But the principle is as relevant for the neighborhoods, churches, and families of today: believing in God does not make one a Christian.

Values

"Good people go to heaven." I believed that statement my entire childhood. My theology as a child could be summed up by "good people go to heaven, and bad people don't, so make sure you're a good boy." Now as an adult, my personal encounters and conversations can verify that this belief is still alive and well, and it is hardly reserved for children. I would argue that my childhood theology is the most common theological position held by self-identified Christian adults in America. There is pride in being seen as good, moral people, and that can function as the chief end of one's family. The belief in heaven is not defined by what is described in the Bible but rather a place in the clouds where you wear white and get to see your loved ones again.

Cultural Christians are the champions of the belief that good people go to heaven, especially since they believe they are the first in line because of their values. Whether God will punish their personal sins, or if they have been forgiven by Christ's saving work on the cross is irrelevant. They go to heaven because they have lived in line with their values and raised nice kids. It is a salvation-by-works worldview. They don't think much about how God factors in, how one knows that heaven is a real place, and what qualifies someone as a good person. But none of those things seem to matter. What matters is being on the nice list, and every Cultural Christian believes they are on it. The Bible is clear that "there is no one righteous, not even one" (Rom. 3:10), but Cultural Christians often don't think in terms of righteous and unrighteous. They think in terms of being a good person as defined by Western standards of values and ethics.

Heritage

Cultural Christians are usually only a generation or two removed from gospel-believing Christians. The heritage of faith in the family can easily be confused with saving faith in Christ. The faith of the grandparents is respected but may be viewed as extreme by the younger generations of the family. So the younger generations ride the coattails of reverent family members and adopt a more comfortable, casual form of that faith.

> **In Cultural Christianity, it is common for one to see himself as being born into Christianity rather than actually being born again.**

I remember being told as a teen at youth camp that "God doesn't have grandchildren." As one who had a Christian grandmother, I needed to hear those words. My grandmother's faithfulness to Christ wouldn't get me in to heaven. God has children, and those children are brought about through faith in Christ (John 1:12–13). A legacy of faith should be celebrated, but a faith that is "inherited" is no faith at all. There is a strong difference between the two. If a faith is only culturally inherited without a response to the saving work of Christ, that legacy, which should be a blessing, can become a barrier. In Cultural Christianity, it is common for one to see himself as being born into Christianity rather than

actually being born again. This false understanding is often culti-
vated in traditional Christian rites of passage.

Rites of Passage

"Emma's baptism is this Sunday," my friend Patrick excitedly
told me when I saw him at a coffee shop. Unsure of what to say, I
replied in an awkwardly high-pitched voice, "Oh, that's great!" I
was caught off guard. I have known this friend for years and have
never known him to go to church, not even on Easter or Christmas Eve. But six weeks after their baby girl was born, he and his
wife went to the church where Patrick was raised (and his parents
are still active members) for Emma to have her infant baptism.

That was over a year ago and they haven't been back since.

Cultural Christianity is perplexing. Patrick believed he was
doing something noble and was excited to tell me about this cer-
emonial religious milestone, since I'm his friend and I'm a pastor.
Their family participated in a rite of passage driven by a desire to
be good parents.

Now, an opportunity for sharing the gospel with Patrick is
wide open for me. There is an easy conversation to start by asking
the honest question of "Why?" That is not a "gotcha" question,
but is often the key to engaging an unsaved Christian friend in
a gospel conversation by using a rite of passage. Timing matters,
and posing the question immediately might have done more
harm than good. A follow-up conversation allows me to ask how
it went, see some pictures he has on his phone from that day, and
engage in a conversation. The probability is that a Cultural Christian will believe that participating in these rites of passage places
them in good standing with God.

Rites of passage for others could include a first communion,
confirmation, baptism by immersion as a young child, or even

saying the "sinner's prayer." Looking back to these moments as adults can be a barrier to understanding the gospel, if genuine conversion did not take place, and these barriers provide false assurance.

Ignorance

Many Cultural Christians simply don't know the difference between what they believe and true Christianity. The only difference they detect with their Christian friends is that they are just "really into church" or "very religious." When it comes to the need to believe the gospel and repent, it may be that they don't know because they've never been told. Cultural Christians may not know the difference between the mainline Protestant church they attend on holidays and the gospel-preaching church next door. They're not technically an unreached people group, but they often lack exposure to biblical preaching. Yet ignorance is not bliss when it comes to authentic Christian faith. It causes them to miss the gospel altogether. Barriers such as belief, values, heritage, and rites of passage fuel the ignorance and allow for a religion to exist that claims Christianity, but not Christ.

Questions for
Discussion and Reflection

- We considered how generic theistic belief, good values,
  religious heritage, Christian rites of passage, and lack of
  knowledge of the true gospel can be barriers to reaching
  Cultural Christians. Can you think of others? *Church
  doctrine*
- Can you remember what barriers in your own life someone
  had to overcome to share the gospel with you? Or, now, for
  maturing Christians, what barriers keep you from healthy
  reliance on God? *Church doctrine*

  *There is no perfect church & no
  perfect pastor*

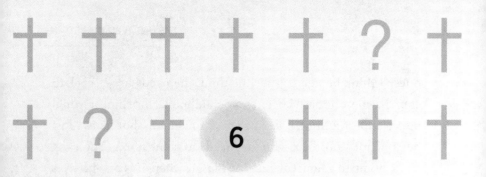

False Assurance:
Once Saved, Always Saved

He asked his first disciples, and he has asked every
disciple since, to give him their thoughtful and total
commitment. Nothing less than this will do.
—JOHN STOTT

"But I know he's okay, because 'once saved, always saved.'" These
were the words of a concerned father, during a conversation we
had about the adult son he claimed was "running from the Lord."

"We raised him right. We were at church every time the doors
were open and he asked Jesus into his heart when he was eight
years old," he continued. "It would mean a lot to me if you talked
to him about coming back to church. I think he would go to your
church."

It was an awkward conversation for me. Little did the man
know his son's friends had been having spiritual conversations
with him and inviting him to church for years. There really had
never been, to my knowledge, any claim of gospel belief, repentance, or any evidence whatsoever of faith in Christ. Sadly, his dad

doesn't think he needs Jesus; he thinks he needs to get back to church, where he hasn't been since childhood. I too think it would be a wonderful thing if he got "back to church," but he is a lost person, not a prodigal who just needs to come home. You can't come home to a house if you don't know where it is or who lives there.

Religious Rites of Passage

A doctrine I believe to be essential in understanding our salvation in Christ is "the perseverance of the saints" or "eternal security," which is sometimes referred to as "once saved, always saved." Theologian Wayne Grudem defines the perseverance of the saints as "the means that all those who are truly born again will be kept by God's power and will persevere as Christians until the end of their lives, and that only those who persevere until the end have been truly born again."[1]

To those who were *truly* born again, Jesus gave great words of assurance concerning their salvation: "This is the will of him who sent me: that I should lose none of those he has given me but should raise them up on the last day" (John 6:39). If you believe that God's will is perfect, and that Jesus isn't a failure in carrying out the Father's will, you know He is not exaggerating. Jesus promised that nobody is able to snatch His sheep out of the Father's hand (John 10:28). Those in Christ have been given salvation. It is a gift, "eternal life that God, who cannot lie, promised before time began" (Titus 1:2). Salvation is based on God's work and promise, and that is not reserved for the moment of being born again, but also remaining in Christ until the end. The Christian can claim with the apostle Paul in confidence, "I am sure of this, that he who started a good work in you will carry it on to completion until the day of Christ Jesus" (Phil. 1:6).

Sadly, this beautiful biblical doctrine, meant to provide the believer assurance and confidence in the redemptive work of Christ, can cause someone to falsely think their children are eternally secure without realizing they may be "unsaved Christians." I know someone who had this mindset, and his reasoning for assurance was that his son asked Jesus into his heart at age eight. This is a common occurrence with Christian families whose adult sons or daughters were raised in the church but do not follow Christ. Can a child genuinely believe the gospel, trust in Christ, and repent of his sins? Certainly. But putting one's assurance in a prayer recited in childhood or an act such as completing a confirmation class may lead to false assurance as an adult and also keep others from seeing one as in need of evangelism.

Overemphasizing a prayer or rite of passage can blind one to the primary calls to salvation, repentance, and faith. When parents insist their adult son or daughter is a Christian because of a childhood prayer or church milestone, they can miss an opportunity to share Christ. Consequently, they can push their child further away from saving faith by creating gospel confusion. This results in a faulty understanding of the gospel in the child and a faulty view of eternal security in the parent, who insists a loved one is a Christian because of their familiarity or background with the church.

> **Overemphasizing a prayer or rite of passage can blind one to the primary calls to salvation, repentance, and faith.**

When Christian families admonish unbelieving relatives to "come back home" to a Christian lifestyle, the principle being practiced and preached is that the individual merely needs to get back to church with his family, or stop drinking so much beer, or get out of that bad relationship, etc. While these are good goals, they should be motivated by genuine faith in Christ rather than guilt or familial expectations.

These situations often require strategic and intentional evangelism. If you were sharing the gospel with an openly non-Christian friend, you wouldn't expect him to immediately attend church, get involved in a ministry team, and give up his lifestyle with ease. It takes investment, intentionality, patience, and time. The same is true for our family members who are not believers—even if we know they have had exposure to the truth for years. While it is a sobering moment to admit that your son or daughter—who grew up in the church, asked Jesus into their heart, and was even baptized—might be a lost person in need of salvation, the embarrassment or failure you may feel is in no way as serious as the reality of being dead in one's sins and needing to be made alive in Christ (Eph. 2:1–4).

Marks of Genuine Conversion

In an interview about his book *Stop Asking Jesus into Your Heart*, J. D. Greear stated that

> surveys show that more than 50% of people in the U.S. have prayed a sinner's prayer and think they're going to heaven because of it, even though there is no detectable difference in their lifestyles from those outside of the church. Thus . . . so many people are assured of a salvation they give no evidence of possessing on the basis of a prayer ritual they didn't understand.[2]

A study by the Barna group found that 35 percent of Americans eighteen years or older claim to have "made a personal commitment to Jesus," yet further questions reveal that only 7 percent hold orthodox views on topics including biblical inerrancy, salvation, and evangelism.[3] The response to this reality is that "we need to preach salvation by repentance before God and faith in the finished work of Christ."[4]

In the parable of the sower, Jesus addressed those who never show any fruit of their claimed salvation. After telling the parable, He explains it in detail to His disciples:

> "When anyone hears the word about the kingdom and doesn't understand it, the evil one comes and snatches away what was sown in his heart. This is the one sown along the path. And the one sown on rocky ground—this is one who hears the word and immediately receives it with joy. But he has no root and is short-lived. When distress or persecution comes because of the word, immediately he falls away. Now the one sown among the thorns—this is one who hears the word, but the worries of this age and the deceitfulness of wealth choke the word, and it becomes unfruitful. But the one sown on the good ground—this is one who hears and understands the word, who does produce fruit and yields: some a hundred, some sixty, some thirty times what was sown." (Matt. 13:19–23)

Jesus gives us a guide for what true conversion looks like for the Christian: *hear the word, understand the word, produce fruit.* These are the marks or evidence of genuine conversion. And let's not forget that this is possible only by grace, not human effort. Jesus called for fruit, and James declared that a life without it possesses no true faith at all (James 2:14). The Spirit brings fruit and repentance, which stem from believing the gospel by faith.

Another category of sown seed is one in which the gospel was heard, and may have appeared to be understood, but was short-lived. A troubling reality in much of evangelical life is that convincing someone they are saved seems to take precedence over making sure someone actually *is* saved. This must change. Somehow questioning another person's salvation became taboo in evangelical culture, when it could possibly be one of the most loving things you can do for another; it could mean the difference between seeds that sprout and bloom and seeds that are snatched away. Those who hear the Word, understand the Word, and bear fruit can be assured that as they work out their salvation, it is a salvation guaranteed in Christ. God is the author and perfecter of the Christian's faith (Heb. 12:2).

Let me clarify that we are not on a witch-hunt for falsely assured believers and should never disparage someone struggling to follow Christ and failing. None of us is the Holy Spirit, and we cannot know who is saved and who is not. All we can know are the marks given in Scripture for true, saving faith. If someone shows consistent fruitlessness and unrepentance, it may be appropriate to confront them in love. But even then, the Christian must remember their own need for grace and their own inability to "fix" anyone.

> A troubling reality in much of evangelical life is that convincing someone they are saved seems to take precedence over making sure someone actually is saved.

System Failure

It is common to look at a process within an organization and conclude there was a "system failure" somewhere along the way. There was a glitch, or a breakdown, or something within the organization that was causing issues—and once detected, addressed, and changed, the organization can flourish. Many churches have a "glitch in the system" in pushing for a decision for Christ without a true explanation to bring about understanding. True assurance comes from properly understanding the gospel and from the fruit it produces. God wants the believer to have assurance, and He told us in His Word He wants His followers to know they have eternal life (1 John 5:13). With such assurance available, why would we want to rush someone to a decision or milestone such as baptism or a Christian rite of passage, without making sure they not only heard the gospel but also have a clear understanding that is going to lead them in their assurance to bear fruit?

For this reason, pastors and churches should invest in quality discipleship efforts, making sure that people are not just pressured to a momentous decision but invited into a lifelong journey of becoming more like Christ and walking with a body of believers (more about this in chapter 9).

As a pastor in a college town, I often hear things like, "I was baptized at a young age, but I don't think it was my decision. I was doing it to please my parents." They don't mean it was forced on them, but that the process they went through was centered on a rite of passage rather than understanding the gospel and responding with repentance and faith. The usual mode of operation is that the parents will meet with the pastor; he will ask the child, often barely old enough to ride a bike, if he has asked Jesus into his heart and wants to be baptized. I have never heard of a child answering "no" in that conversation, and you can imagine the reason why, given the pressure and formality of the environment. When I talk to other pastors, I find that they too have numerous accounts of people wanting to get "baptized again," because they were baptized as a child and either don't remember it, or believe they have actually come to understand the gospel since that childhood church milestone. That leaves the pastor in quite the predicament, as there is only one baptism, but the description given by the individual alludes to an elementary-school-age version of an infant baptism, which isn't tied to conversion at all.

There are certainly adults living for Christ today who point to their decision to trust in Christ as a young child and their baptism as a second grader as their public profession of faith, and this should not be minimized. The more important aspect of conversion is the object of faith, and that is the Lord Jesus Christ. There is a time when someone believes the gospel by confessing Christ and repenting of sin, and this is significant. The glitch in the system is when weight is placed on the experience of that moment, rather than the person and saving work of Christ.

As I think back to the brief conversation with my friend's father, I am reminded of this verse from 1 John: "They went out from us, but they did not belong to us; for if they had belonged to us, they would have remained with us" (2:19). I am not the judge of who is "with us" or not, but I know the Prodigal Son came home and wonder if my friend ever will, or if he even knows where home is located. If he doesn't, perhaps he is whom John is describing. But I will know one thing for certain: he needs to be saved, not assured. Until that day, if the Lord allows, I am going to pray the Lord saves his soul and will share the gospel with him as if he is someone who has never heard the gospel before. For my own children, I want them to continue to hear, understand on

their own, and bear fruit in repentance. These are more important
to me than church moments or milestones and will make those
moments even sweeter, because it won't be a sugar substitute but
the real thing. The doctrine of perseverance and eternal security
are treasures for the believer; we just need to make sure we aren't
banking on fool's gold.

Questions for
Discussion and Reflection

- Ask yourself again the question from chapter 1: If someone
  asked me how I know I'm a Christian, what would I say?
  Am I tempted to point to a religious rite of passage or an
  emotional moment?

  [handwritten: I trust in Jesus' works & His word. See my works that I am following Jesus. It's not a point but a life long process.]

- If you have trusted in Christ for the forgiveness of your sins,
  how does it calm your soul to know that you are purchased
  by the blood of Jesus and held by God alone?

  [handwritten: It is well with my soul. Jesus has conquered death. He is at work in my life]

The Country Club Church:
How Lax Church Membership Fosters Cultural Christianity

As sinful human beings we have an instinctual,
compulsive bias toward forms of religion that
we ourselves can create and control.
—OS GUINNESS

Is it possible for Bible-believing churches to unintentionally allow Cultural Christianity to flourish in their own congregations?

A church membership inquiry several years ago led me to realize it is easier than I had ever considered. "What changes on Monday if I join the church and become a member on Sunday? I just don't see the point." That question stumped me, and it came during our first-ever membership class at the church I planted. *Does anything actually change?* I thought, as I tried to scrounge up an answer in front of about twenty people who now were probably wondering the same thing. I don't remember what I said, but I know it wasn't very good. I had no quality answer to give, because in our church, at that point, there really was no change. After being flustered for the rest of the Q&A, I started thinking about the question and realized it was not only a great question but also a crucial one.

What does it mean to be a member of a church? For us, as I look back to our early years, it only meant we were the church you said you were going to come to on Sunday morning, until you decided to go someplace else. As I considered the Cultural Christian climate of the city we had set out to reach, I came to the humbling realization that I had been unaware that our model of church membership was the very type of church practice that allows Cultural Christianity to flourish. We had it in place because we thought we were supposed to, I guess, but we couldn't really describe why it mattered. Unsaved Christians thrive where church membership means nothing and is available to all, without anything changing the day after you "sign up."

> **Our model of church membership was the very type of church practice that allows Cultural Christianity to flourish.**

What's the Point?

It's easy for processes within churches to become formalities. In many traditional Southern Baptist churches, for example, the method of becoming a member is to walk forward during an invitation at the conclusion of a worship service and join the church by filling out a card with personal contact information. If people come forward to join the church as members, they will simply indicate whether they are joining by a transfer of letter (coming from another church), a "statement of faith" (they are already claiming to be believers), or baptism (they have to be baptized by immersion to become a member). After meeting them, the pastor will introduce them to the church by announcing, "This is Justin and Amanda Thompson, and they are joining our church today by statement of faith, all who receive them say 'amen.'" And now officially, Justin and Amanda are members.

Other denominations or churches require aspiring members to take a class as part of a process where they learn about the church's beliefs and history, and meet some of the staff. There are also those who declare an infant to be a member after their baptism, but regardless of the process, the question of "what changes" still too often cannot be answered. Those who can answer the question are the exception. These scenarios are not exaggerations or extreme examples. This happens in churches all over America, and the logical follow-up question is what I heard in our first-ever membership class: "What's the point?"

Much of the American megachurch craze was built on seeker-sensitive models attracting "de-churched" people. In these churches, often membership didn't exist, or required nothing, or consisted of systemized assembly-line baptisms and a sign-up list called church membership. Often that membership meant less than joining a local gym, book club, or Facebook group. Churches that forgo membership (as is the case in some seeker-sensitive churches) misunderstand the local church as designed by God.

It is important to remember that unsaved Christians are not seekers. Church (with its traditions, institutions, and programming) is not foreign to them. "Joining" a church by becoming a member was likely part of their upbringing and a familiar practice. It is fair to say that church membership is an unspoken expectation for Cultural Christians, even if attendance is sparse.

This expectation could be internal (i.e., the "right thing to do") or a felt pressure from Christian relatives. For others it is a rite of passage, especially after having children, to sign the kids up for confirmation or baptism to continue the family tradition. I have a marginally churched friend who drove eight hours to his parents' hometown to have his infant baptized in a church that was not his own. Cultural Christianity is a strange bird, indeed. Even if one is seldom seen at church, it is important in Cultural Christianity that one can at least claim a church as his own.

Making Membership Meaningful Again

I would rather have someone be an "attender" and know they are not a church member than be an official member and unsure of what that means. The good news is that meaningful church membership cuts through the very fabric of Cultural Christianity. Church membership with low or no expectations accommodates Cultural Christians. But being a member of a local church as it was intended means one is part of local covenant community of faith in Jesus Christ. With that definition, Cultural Christianity cannot exist. False believers will either flee the particular church altogether, or the light will go on in their minds, and they will see that something is missing in their lives as compared to true believers: faith and repentance. This difference needs to be clear and obvious. Belonging to a church is more, but certainly not less, than this starting point, since "New Testament churches were covenanted communities of individuals who had embraced the gospel."[1]

Faith, Repentance, and Membership

As strange as it sounds, for some churches, faith in Christ is not a prerequisite to church membership. This is usually the case in theologically liberal (often mainline) Protestant churches. As a pastor, I would need to drink Nyquil to sleep if I was leading a church where one could be part of the church without knowing Christ, but this is commonplace in Cultural Christianity. Churches that require members to be genuine believers are more concerned with an individual actually understanding the gospel than they are adding someone to the church or being inclusive. This is commonly referred to as "regenerate church membership."

While every evangelical pastor would likely claim that someone understanding the gospel is their first priority, church membership models often communicate the opposite, especially when joining the church is as easy as filling out personal information on a card. Different churches may have different requirements for church membership, but one non-negotiable should be that one has to believe the gospel of Jesus Christ by faith and repent of sin. The reason for this is simple: love for God and love for our neighbor. The church is loving God by taking His gospel and commands seriously, and loving their neighbor by wanting them to actually know the gospel of Jesus Christ and not be misled that they are Christians simply because they joined a church.

The Church: Universal and Local

While a worship gathering is open to all people, being a member of a local church should be reserved for those who are first part of the universal church, where membership is informal and comes by faith and repentance. If one is not part of the church universal, it is negligent to allow that person to be part of the church local. Regenerate church membership begins with evangelism, and the opportunity available to lead one to faith in Christ by requiring regenerate church membership cannot be overstated. In my experience at the church I pastor, the clearest

> **If one is not part of the church universal, it is negligent to allow them to be part of the church local.**

path to one believing the gospel and being baptized has been realization during a membership meeting that they needed to be saved. Many people walk into the membership meeting as their personal rite of passage and leave realizing they need much more than a "church home"—they need to be forgiven of their sins and trust in Christ.

It has always puzzled me how a Cultural Christian can sit in a church service where the gospel is clearly preached and still remain as they are, feeling no disconnect. It can create immense frustration and impatience, especially when they come up to me following the service to tell me how much they loved the sermon. Usually my internal response is, "I was talking to you . . . when are you going to get it?!" I have to remind myself of my own story and God's patience with me, and how that mercy continues in my life daily. But seeing my friends at our church services brings me great hope, since their cultural wirings to "join a church" allow for one-on-one conversations about what this means and does not mean. And this begins with what it means to be a Christian. Allowing someone to join a church as a member without being sure that person understands the saving work of Jesus Christ—and has responded by faith and repentance—is allowing them to join a covenant community when they actually belong in an evangelistic conversation. The demands of the Christian life, expressed in the covenant community of the local church, begin to make sense and apply when, and only when, one is born again.

Church members are those who "voluntarily make to God

and to one another . . . their basic moral and spiritual commit-
ments and the practice of their faith."[2] The call to the Christian
life is a call to believe the gospel, repent of sin, and follow Christ
with others. To put it plainly, this is church membership. An unre-
generate person cannot and should not have to understand such
a reality that exists for a Christian. Rather, he needs to be made
aware of his sin and need for Christ.

This also matters greatly for the witness in the community of
the church. Unbelievers know
when their friends who claim to
be Christian don't actually take
their faith seriously. It is detri-
mental to the mission of God in
a community when unbelievers
see little distinction between
themselves and friends who are
associated with a church. Chris-
tians are called by Christ to let their lights shine before others
(Matt. 5:16), and this is impossible to accomplish if they don't
actually possess the light to shine.

> **Unbelievers know when their friends who claim to be Christian don't actually take their faith seriously.**

Church Membership in Scripture

The question I fielded back at our first-ever membership meeting
forced me to evaluate what I actually believed about being part of
a church. I had to face the painful truth that I, as the pastor of the
church, had little substance around my convictions about church
membership. In a town like mine, saturated with Cultural Christianity, we were helping to fuel the fire by not translating what we
were preaching from the pulpit about the local church into life
and practice. To borrow a saying from my Texas friends, we were

"all hat and no cattle." This made us a safe space for Cultural Christianity—everything we set out not to be when we first planted.
I do not mean that a Cultural Christian should feel unwelcome
at the church, but rather that they should be uncomfortable by
the glaring gap between what Christianity is and what it is not.
Reaching Cultural Christianity was my proclaimed passion when
we first cast the vision for the church, and from the start, without
even realizing it, I was helping it flourish in my own congregation.
Something had to change.

First, I had to ask what the Bible has to say about church membership, and that can be a complicated task. The words "church
membership" or "joining a church" are not explicitly in the Bible,
which results in a common misconception that the Bible doesn't
address them at all. But the absence of terminology doesn't mean
the practice is missing. Paul writes his New Testament letters to
local churches. Receiving and understanding his letters apart
from being part of a church body would be like receiving a parent
newsletter from a school your child doesn't attend. It would be
random and make no sense. Being part of the church was understood as the context for the encouragement, instruction, correc-
tion, doctrine, and truth they received. If this was God's model for
His people, I needed to make sure it was our model as well, and
this required making membership meaningful. This began with
regenerate church membership, but that was the starting point
to a healthy church, which must be defined by spiritually healthy
Christians. We then wanted to ensure that joining our local
church meant actually being part of a body, a people. Meaningless
church membership only provides this in theory.

Initial changes we made centered around our belief that discipleship matters and happens best in community. To join our
church now meant you were agreeing to be part of a discipleship

environment with others, covenanted together in the same local church family. Joining a Bible study, or being involved in one of our "growth environments," was now an agreement one made in becoming a member. Christians as part of a local church are called to live their lives among the unbelievers in the city (1 Peter 2:12). In doing so, they should not resemble the unbelieving world, but live distinct lives, hoping to point people to our distinct God. Based on this biblical conviction, becoming a member of our church is an agreement to live one's life in holiness, in order to protect one's own fellowship with God and also our reputation in the community with unbelievers, as followers of Christ. When a member engages in sinful patterns without repentance, the leadership in the church holds that person accountable and hopes to restore them to right fellowship with God and the church, out of love for that church member and the entire church family. Without church membership, there is no true spiritual authority in place for accountability, and this is a detriment to Christian living.

Jesus also called the disciples to serve one another (Matt. 20:28; John 13:14–15). Therefore Christians are called to serve one another within the body of Christ, that is, the church (Eph. 4:16). To be part of a body means to serve that body. This includes volunteering in ministry areas of the church and also serving the church by being a financial contributor who gives generously to the work of the church. Membership carrying the expectation to believe sound doctrine, practice community, strive for holiness, and serve the body of Christ will be too much for an unsaved Christian. Either they will flee or realize that a life of holiness and dedication to Christ is the very thing that has been missing in their idea of being a Christian. As a result of making changes, we saw people either hit the road or step in the baptismal to make professions of faith in Christ. I don't want anyone to leave the church, but would prefer they decide they don't want to be a covenant church member than falsely believe they are part of a church because we had a glorified formality we called church membership. Meaningful church membership is the greatest friend to evangelism and discipleship.

"WHERE IN THE BIBLE DOES IT TALK ABOUT BEING A MEMBER OF A CHURCH?"

Pastor and author David Schrock wrote a helpful article[3] supporting his claim that "membership does not add something extra to the church. It enables the church to be the church, both now and for generations to come," by pointing to the biblical metaphors of the church in Scripture:

1. **The local church is a royal embassy.** Church membership is a visible identification with Christ's kingdom people (Ps. 110; 2 Tim. 2:12). Schrock states that each church is an embassy of the kingdom, and thus personal commitment to a local church publicly identifies a Christian with the King.
2. **The local church is the family of God.** Being a member of a local church is being a member of God's household and His family, as spiritual siblings, together (Matt. 19:29; John 1:12; 1 Tim. 3:15).
3. **We are stones in Christ's temple.** God's people are described as a people built and as living stones (Eph. 2:20; 1 Peter 2:5; 2 Cor. 6:16).
4. **We are Christ's body** (Rom. 12:5; 1 Cor. 12:12–14; Eph. 4:11–16). Schrock writes that the body metaphor replaces a consumer approach to church membership with a

stewardship approach to church membership.

5. **The church is the bride of Christ** (Eph. 5:31–32). Every marriage is designed to be a visible portrait of Christ's union with His church.

These all invoke deep images of belonging: a kingdom, a family, a building block in a larger structure, a part of a body, a bride in a marriage. Membership is not a new invention; it is the basic understanding of how we are to live out our faith together.

Country Club Churches

When one thinks of a "country club church," it usually comes with the negative connotation that the church is stuffy, snooty, and closed off to the community. And we know that's not always the case. But that misidentification is only part of the problem. Country clubs thrive only to the extent that they cater to their members. If the members of the club aren't happy, they will leave for another club across town. If you are employed by a country club, you don't want to commit the unforgivable sin: upsetting the members. This makes sense for a country club with tennis courts and eighteen holes of golf, but in churches, it allows unsaved Christianity to exist unchallenged. Country club churches cater to members and fear people leaving for another church across town. By "catering," I am not referring to actively caring about personal growth in discipleship and sanctification but rather making sure people are never offended. Country club churches rarely call people to repent. I am convinced that a primary reason

> I am convinced that a primary reason Cultural Christianity isn't challenged in some churches is because pastors are afraid those people will leave if offended.

Cultural Christianity isn't challenged in some churches is because pastors are afraid those people will leave if offended.

A church that refuses to call people to die to themselves and follow Christ is going to be full of people who admire and are "cool" with Jesus, as long as He doesn't interfere with their lives. Push beyond the casual admiration of Jesus and the country club church will lose members (who will go pay their annual dues to a different church across town), and that is far too much risk for the pastor running the clubhouse. These churches avoid hard topics, functionally forbid the confrontation of personal sin, and only make expectations related to financial contribution. I do not believe one should offend for the sake of offending, but I am advocating that local churches call people away from themselves and to submission to Christ. Country club churches are the purveyors of moralistic therapeutic deism. These churches might have incredible music in their services, exciting environments for children and youth ministries, and an amazing communicator for a pastor. People receive self-help advice, accompanied by Bible verses that point to a moral and inspiring life.

While I hope people live inspiring lives with good morals, that doesn't require the gospel of Jesus Christ. The greatest preaching instruction I ever received in seminary was, "Never preach a sermon that would still be true if Jesus hadn't died and risen from the grave." A sermon like this, after all, would not be Christian. These sermons are hard to detect, because on the surface, they may include mention of God, faith, and specific Bible verses. What they lack, though, is a clear emphasis on Jesus being the centerpiece and focus of the Bible, and this is significant because life change only truly happens through Jesus Christ. Sermons where Jesus is missing or neglected explain Cultural Christianity in a nutshell: Christianity without Christ, a belief system in which God's love and acceptance are assumed but not defined.

The cure for a country club church is not to care for members less but to care for them more. Loving them more means calling them to what Christ already called them to, and that is Himself. Not to a generic religion, moral code, theism, ethic, family tradition, or therapeutic practice but to an actual belief in and commitment to Jesus Christ as He presented Himself to us in the Scriptures. Gospel clarity might be offensive to some, but it is "the power of God for salvation to everyone who believes" (Rom. 1:16). My friends who are Cultural Christians attend churches where their version of Christianity isn't challenged, and they don't realize it's not Christianity at all. I know firsthand the experience of one who has only known country club church and then hears the actual preaching of the gospel for the first time. You know it when you hear it, and the response is that it's "a lot different than what they say at my church."

Churches trying to reach their community with the gospel should view Cultural Christians walking in the door from another church not as "sheep swapping" or transfer growth but an actual evangelistic opportunity. If you want to reach Cultural Christians, you can't be afraid to believe and say that out loud.

The local church can be an incubator of Cultural Christianity, or a remedy for it. The remedy is a gospel centrality that confronts Cultural Christians with the truth about Christ and themselves.

Questions for
Discussion and Reflection

- Do you see the church primarily as a place to meet your own needs? N e

- Do you get defensive over who gets to be part of your church or make decisions in your church? No

- Do any of these characteristics of a Country Club Christian describe you? No

  Mechurch
  » **Consumeristic.** Feels the church exists primarily for one's own experience. Transactional
  » **Fickle/noncommittal.** Has one foot out the door at current church. Sees church involvement as a one-way commitment: *as long as the church is operating as I believe it should, I will stay.*
  » **Selective generosity.** Will contribute financially to certain mission causes, but often will not personally engage in the mission effort.
  » **Lack of spiritual self-awareness.** Views oneself as a mature Christian, though not growing or becoming more like Jesus. May know the Lord, but needs to be discipled. Immature in the faith but a veteran in church life.

- Are you tempted to cling to comfort at the cost of mission? No Do you avoid messy things like people and ministry? No

Remember that Jesus gave us the Great Commission (Matt. 28:16–20). Jesus' primary call to us is to repent (Matt. 4:17), put faith in Him, and tell the world who He is and what He's done. There's no bench for true followers of Christ.

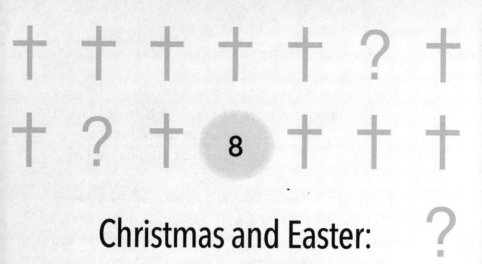

Christmas and Easter:
Moving Beyond Cultural Observance to the Life-Changing Implications

> A man may pine for peace and have no interest in the Prince of Peace. Many who claim they are questing for God are not thirsting for God as He has revealed Himself in Scripture, but only for God as they want Him to be, or for a god who will give them what they want.
> —DONALD WHITNEY

For most churches, Easter and Christmas Eve are the local church versions of the Super Bowl. From small rural churches to suburban megachurches, the crowd will likely be larger on these days than any other services of the year. Catholic churches add extra mass times to the schedule for those days, and church planters bring out extra chairs. It is a picture of everything the church hopes for when it comes to reaching people. It is common for creative teams to design special graphics and social media campaigns for these worship services. Extra volunteers are needed, the band puts in extra time during rehearsal, the pastor is dressed a notch higher on the style scale than his usual attire. In other words, the church goes "all out" for Easter Sunday and Christmas Eve. People are coming, and the church is pumped.

Immediately following these holiday services, many pastors and staff feel a rush and a good kind of exhaustion. But the Sunday following these services is a different story. The extra chairs go away, the extra worship services that were added won't be seen again until the following Easter and Christmas Eve, and the question lingering is, "Who were these people, and where did they go?"

In our second year as a church plant, we decided to go all out for Easter by having our service in a well-known local concert venue. Our church, which at the time consisted of about four hundred people meeting in a high school auditorium, had never been more excited. Church members crafted social media posts inviting friends to come, we sent teams across neighborhoods to invite people, and created all kinds of hype for our Easter service, because we genuinely were that excited. We believed this was our big chance to reach the lost in our community—having our Easter service in this popular local venue was just the ticket and open door we needed for an easy invitation to church. Easter finally came, after weeks of our entire church counting down the days, and more than 1,000 people showed up—1,013 to be exact. It was such a thrill and day of celebration for our church that I will never forget that number. We utilized the opportunity by clearly preaching the gospel and had (from a quality and excellence perspective) the best service we had ever had.

The next day, I sat down with some key leaders in the church to celebrate and figure out what we were going to do the following Sunday when all these new people showed up for church. We went from less than four hundred people at a worship service to 1,013 in one week. We felt like outreach gurus. People loved the service and the buzz around town was very positive, claiming our Easter service was as advertised. The following Sunday, we put out every extra chair we could find in the high school, as we were back at our regular meeting place ready to see the masses come into the door; 398 people showed up for our service—1,013 to 398, in one week. That is almost the same number of people we had the Sunday before Easter. Did our Easter service accomplish nothing? Without a church split or a tropical storm coming over our city at the exact time of our service, we had 61 percent drop-off in just one week. If there was a Mount Rushmore of my most discouraging moments, that Sunday definitely made the list. *What did we do wrong? Did I say something offensive? But I'd heard so much positive feedback! I can understand telling me you "enjoyed the service" to my face, but I was hearing feedback from church members, from their friends!* While "numbers" are not the sole focus of our church, this destroyed our morale and made me feel like the coach of a team that was ranked preseason #1 and then didn't make a bowl game.

Cultural Christians and the Holidays

Years later, we still have a very large church gathering at Easter. It's usually double the attendance of the average Sunday throughout the year. And the Sunday after Easter always reveals a vast drop-off, but we no longer freak out. We now know what Easter Sunday is (in a cultural sense) and whom it attracts. Unbelievers don't usually go to church on Easter Sunday. It is a stretch to see Easter as an outreach that is going to grow the church, because outside of an Easter egg hunt and a basket full of jelly beans awaiting the kids, unbelievers don't care about Easter. For them, the holiday is a glorified celebration of spring that happens to be an American tradition, and the resurrection of Jesus Christ is irrelevant. They most likely aren't going to church on Easter because that has nothing to do with their family practice of the holiday. Hearing that a church is doing a big "Easter extravaganza" on Sunday morning wouldn't make them go to an Easter service any more than a special Ramadan gathering would entice a non-Muslim to put the family in the car and drive to the mosque. Easter as an outreach (in the traditional understanding of the word) is overblown and overrated. It is not unchurched people who show up to church for Easter in droves—it is *unsaved Christians* who walk in the door.

The reason most churches see Easter as the largest crowd of the year by a significant margin isn't because unbelievers heard the service was going to be awesome. The spiked numbers are due to the Cultural Christians showing up and bringing family members. They may come back to church before next Easter, but it might not be for months, because it simply isn't a priority in their lives. But Easter is important because everyone who claims they attend a church actually shows up at the same time. For the Cultural Christian family, church on Easter is just what you do. It would take hurricane-force winds or flash flooding to keep these families from putting on their pastels and getting to church before going to Grandma's for ham. The following Sunday, though, it is back to normal, and regular church attendance falls way down the list of priorities. Maybe they'll be at church on Mother's Day if Mom puts on the guilt trip.

Christmas Eve services are the same. An unbelieving family doesn't put pressure on the adult children to bring the grandkids to sit next to Nana in their matching sweaters for the church Christmas Eve service. In an unbelieving family, Nana doesn't go to church at all, and Christmas has no effect on that. The family pressure she places on everyone is to be in town and take a family picture and celebrate the holiday season together without any need of the Bethlehem manger or shepherds. For Cultural Christians, though, going to church on Christmas Eve is as expected as hanging stockings and decorating a Christmas tree. You can bet those families will be at the service, holding their candles in the air as they sing "Silent Night."

It is vital to realize that, with Cultural Christianity, holiday church tradition takes priority over the understanding of the holiday. Yet we can still use the holidays to preach the gospel unapologetically to Cultural Christians. While the practice of only going to church once or twice a year can be frustrating for pastors, church leaders, and Christians living on mission, there is a significant ministry opportunity that occurs when unsaved Christians simply walk in the door to a local church worship service to celebrate two of the most significant events in all of the Christian faith: the incarnation and the resurrection. It is easy and far too common for churches to throw away the opportunity to use the tradition of holidays to help Cultural Christians understand exactly what they are doing by "observing" these foundational Christian celebrations. I pray that I don't squander the chance to provide clarity to a willing and present audience.

"Happy Easter! We haven't seen you guys since Christmas Eve. Good to have you back," a pastor chuckles as he opens his sermon. While the pastor probably thinks he is challenging people to be in church more often, or maybe just trying to be funny, he is unknowingly communicating the wrong message: that what the people need is to be in church more frequently. Of course the pastor doesn't believe one is saved by their works but has nonetheless cast guilt on the "Christmas and Easter crowd."

I believe the weekend gathering is a crucial aspect of discipleship. But unsaved Christians need forgiveness of sins, not better church attendance. Pressuring people into being at church reinforces the mentality of salvation by church attendance or salvation by works. Genuine believers certainly need to prioritize gathering with their local church (Heb. 10:25). And it is obviously beneficial for Cultural Christians to attend church if the gospel is faithfully preached, but they need to be forgiven of their sins by believing the gospel, repenting, and being made alive in Christ. "I know I need to get to church more" is a favorite line for a Cultural Christian to use when feeling guilty, and we must make sure that we do not communicate a message that leads them to believe that church attendance is the solution for their life or that it is the message of Christianity. The goal is for them to see their need for Christ, not church attendance. The church must make sure it provides no confusion.

The Strangeness of Cultural Christianity

While an unsaved Christian's greatest need in life is not church attendance, the mere fact that they typically attend such a specific type of church service is bizarre. While it takes some savvy to acknowledge that without making them feel unwelcome, I try to help them see how ludicrous Cultural Christianity is, especially on Christmas and Easter. Consider the very events for which they join us to celebrate and the tremendous disconnect that exists. On Christmas Eve, they acknowledge that the long-awaited Messiah has been born; that the climax of the entire storyline of the Old Testament and the basis for all understanding of the New Testament is found in a manger. Here they are, dressed up, sitting with the family for this special service centered on the birth of Jesus Christ, Savior of the world.

In my Christmas Eve sermons, I make it a priority to challenge everyone in the room to not acknowledge or even celebrate Christmas but to actually *respond* to Christmas. "Think about what you're doing tonight. You are holding a candle proclaiming that Jesus is the light of the world. You just knew every word to a song about angels singing 'glory to the newborn king' and rejoicing about 'God and sinners reconciled.'" While I try to have tact and not be condescending or judgmental, I want the Cultural Christian to see how bizarre it is if the day after Christmas nothing changes besides the Christmas decorations being put away. We may joke about the neighbor who leaves the Christmas lights up year round, but in a figurative sense, Christians should likewise be responding to Christmas year round if we really do believe the words of the carols and the world-altering significance of the nativity scene. The bottom line is that Christmas is a strange thing for a Cultural Christian to celebrate, and I want them to be confronted with that reality *for their ultimate benefit*.

> **In a figurative sense, Christians should likewise be responding to Christmas year round if we really do believe the words of the carols and the world-altering significance of the nativity scene.**

Sadly, in the name of tradition and good tidings, a Cultural Christian can have all the comforts of the Christmas season without being confronted with their need to follow the very One whose birth they acknowledge. This paradox hit me while sitting in a coffee shop writing a sermon during Christmastime. At this secular chain in a suburban area, customers were sitting and tapping their feet to a jazzy version of "Joy to the World." Not a generic song about jingle bells or walking in a winter wonderland but a song specifically about Jesus Christ. I looked around and no one seemed offended—I even caught a few people singing along about earth receiving her King. It made me wonder if they would ever play a song about Jesus in the month of February or how the customers would react if they suddenly heard "In Christ Alone" play across the store. Cultural Christianity is indeed strange, and Christmas is one of the greatest opportunities to ask questions of our Cultural Christian friends who seem to be most excited about the incarnation of the Son of God.

In the church, we need to make sure people understand what they are claiming to celebrate at Christmastime, and that thing is not winter or Hallmark movies. The truth of Christmas must confront them as it did Simeon, who, after waiting a lifetime for the promised Messiah, responded to the birth of Christ: "for my eyes have seen your salvation" (Luke 2:30). The angel Gabriel told Mary that this baby she would deliver "will be great and will be called the Son of the Most High, and the Lord God will give him the throne of his father David. He will reign over the house of Jacob forever, and his kingdom will have no end" (1:32–33).

Yet the Cultural Christian response to this news is to travel home for the holidays and get dressed up for Christmas Eve? I know atheists who do that with their families at Christmastime. But people who get defensive over the right to portray Jesus in a nativity scene and then live the rest of their lives like He doesn't matter are giving us an open window to lean in with questions. Behind sermons and church services, Christians must have the courage and love to engage in the "forbidden" talk of religion at the dinner table and ask exactly what these loved ones are celebrating and why it matters. The answer may confirm that they want sweet baby Jesus to functionally remain in the manger. He seems a lot more harmless there. After all, "no crying he makes." (Due to that line, I've always wondered if the writer of "Away in a Manger" ever even met a newborn baby.)

Don't Get Drunk on Easter

Cultural Christian Easter observance is even stranger. Not the fact that it is in the top tier of holidays observed but that Cultural Christians can extract any meaning from it and abandon the implications of that meaning. The apostle Paul thought the resurrection was such a big deal that he claimed if Jesus had not been raised, the entire Christian faith is in vain (1 Cor. 15:14). The resurrection of Jesus Christ does many things, but chief among them might be proving Christmas was no hoax, and that it deserves much more than figgy pudding and halls decked with boughs of holly. How much more, then, is Easter deserving of more than one day in our entire year?

I was first exposed to a Cultural Christian understanding of Easter during a spring break trip to the beach while I was a high school student, not long after my Christian conversion. Each year for spring break, the majority of my class would head down to one of the beaches closest to my hometown to enjoy our week off from school together. Everyone would chip in to cover the cost of renting a beach house, and a few "cool" parents would come as chaperones. We would have several houses along the beach full of high school students and one designated cool mom per house. This particular spring break, Easter fell over the first weekend we were at the beach. On Friday and Saturday, people were drinking a lot of beer, and the beach was full of drunken high school students, while the cool moms pretended they had no clue. It was essentially a beer-themed weekend, except for one day—Sunday. Nobody engaged in any underaged drinking whatsoever. I was curious as to why. Had the crew run out of beer? Did they get caught with fake IDs while buying the drinks at the gas station? I asked one of my buddies why today everyone had switched to bottled water and Diet Coke, and he looked offended I would even ask the question. "Come on, bro. We can't get wasted on Easter. That's just messed up." But when the sun rose on Monday morning and Easter was over, the drinking came back full speed.

This sounds like an extreme example, but there is an adult version of this all around us: a culture in which people can acknowledge Easter on the official Sunday of the year, and then Monday return to a life unaffected by the history-altering event of Christ's resurrection. "Since Jesus rose from the grave, let's not get drunk on Sunday. Wait until Monday." This is Cultural Christianity on display. There's a difference between faith as verbal affirmation and faith as conviction. The former dresses up for Easter, the latter is clothed in Christ (Rom. 13:14).

The Disconnect

When preaching on Easter Sunday, the pastor has to know that many of the people present did not get coerced into being at church that day. There may even be unsaved Christians in that room who are pumped to see what the band plays or what the pastor talks about. The fact is, for many Cultural Christians, Easter church attendance is a non-negotiable priority. Cultural Christians celebrate Easter, but they are indifferent to the resurrection. What an opportunity to preach the gospel! As pastors, we can respond faithfully to this opportunity by challenging (in truth and love) how strange and bizarre it is to celebrate Easter if on Monday everything will be back to normal. We can explain how, for followers of Christ, Easter changes everything. No matter when a believer came to faith, there's not a single thing in our lives that isn't impacted by the fact that Jesus rose from the grave and is now seated at the right hand of the Father (Eph. 1:20).

While there is much to be said about the warmth that holidays bring (and how that is in itself an opportunity to point to heaven), I've never been able to figure out why Christmas and Easter would be the "can't miss" church services for the Cultural Christian. What we acknowledge and celebrate on those days are not conventional or widely acceptable things. We acknowledge that a God-Man was born and then that He was brutally murdered and raised from the dead. These are not normal things!

This has to create some sort of disconnect in the mind of a Cultural Christian, unless churches don't preach to that disconnect. In their sermon preparation, pastors should keep in mind that Cultural Christians come out in full force on these days because no self-respecting "Christian" would miss church on Christmas or Easter, right? Sure, we could blame the disconnect on the commercialization of these holidays, but the reality is that today in America, you can celebrate the incarnation and resurrection of the Son of God, without having to believe those climactic biblical events matter at all to your life. These Christian holidays (in their American context) are creeping closer to the "celebration" of St. Patrick's Day, excluding perhaps the added warm, fuzzy feelings of Christmas and the emphasis of being with family on Easter.

PROFILE: Christmas-and-Easter Christians

◈ **Sentimentality is king.** Families must spend these days together, even if various members go the rest of the year without speaking. These gatherings are mandatory. Missing church is not an option.

◈ **Faith is not necessary for the celebrations.** Christmas and Easter are just the December and April stops on the year-long holiday train, following pumpkins, valentines, fireworks, and back-to-school shopping.

◈ **They are committed to tradition.** They want to keep Christ in Christmas. They want these holidays to remain special, even if they don't know why. They prepare, commit, plan, etc.

◈ **There is a disconnect.** Like other holidays, when the calendar changes, the hype is gone and there is no remaining impact on their lives.

In much of the Western world, Christmas has a felt importance, but it's more about being with family than about the arrival of an eternal King. In Cultural Christianity, it's like Russell Moore has said: "always Mardi Gras and never Easter."[1] The warm, fuzzy quality of Christmas and the social pressure of gathering for Easter go unquestioned by most.

Here's an example of a "Christmas-and-Easter Christian" family:

- Susan can't wait for her kids to arrive for the Christmas weekend. December 24th is the only time the family goes to church together all year, and it's always so special. Nana makes her famous oatmeal cookies, the grandkids get Christmas pajamas, and they always sit around the piano while Uncle John plays some carols.

- Melissa has made sure all the preparations are complete. Baby Jesus is on the mantle. She's bought the entire extended family tickets to the Christmas cantata at the local church, and the playroom is ready for all the cousins to watch Charlie Brown and hear Linus read the story of Christ's birth. She's hoping nobody brings up religion again this year because no one sees eye to eye, and she can't handle another family drama.

- Jason works in the city and only sees his family a few times a year, but he takes the week off of work to drive 400 miles to be home for Christmas. He would consider himself an atheist, he guesses, but the holidays are an understood imperative.

You have likely encountered a family like this one. A good entry to conversation is to politely question the point of it all:

- Why did you get ashes on your forehead? What does that mean?

- What is the significance of Jesus' birth? What is celebrated in the nativity?

- Why is it important to spend the holidays with your family?

The Opportunity

When I first started pastoring, I believed Easter and Christmas Eve were the days to reach unbelievers. It took me time to learn that these are actually the days to reach people who think they *are* believers. They walk in the door of local churches on those days without any effort of an outreach campaign. It is the easiest evangelism opportunity most churches will have in terms of unsaved people coming to a church service without any effort on the church's part. The question is: Will they head home for a family meal after the service still thinking they are fine, or will they finally understand that these events (on which the entire church rises or falls) change everything? Christmas and Easter call for faith and repentance as a response to the reality of Jesus Christ as the promised Messiah who conquered sin and death through His death and resurrection.

Gospel conversations with Cultural Christian friends and family can be less forced and awkward during these Christian holidays because the purpose of these holidays is undeniable. Believers should look for opportunities to discuss the church service and ask what others believe about the significance of Christ being born. Leading up to Easter, as friends gather for a neighborhood Easter egg hunt, there is an open door to invite friends to church who are already acknowledging something about the holiday. If someone is already observing this holiday willingly, you've got a starting point for conversation. As believers grow in understanding how and why these holidays are a strange fit for nominal Christians, we'll be more urgent and comfortable to press into the personal disconnect it must cause for those who think about the true meanings of these days and yet ignore the implications.

Starting Points

The birth of Jesus Christ confronts American culture each December. It may be known as "the holiday season" but the nativity is unavoidable in even the most secular cities and is actually invited in the celebrations and traditions of Cultural Christians. Even the children of Cultural Christians will likely watch Linus take the stage at the Christmas play during *A Charlie Brown Christmas* to quote Luke 2 and tell everyone "what Christmas is all about." The nativity is everywhere, and with the nativity comes the incarnation of Christ and the gospel. Christmas should make the Cultural Christian uncomfortable rather than make them feel the "holiday spirit."

Ask pointed questions that force a disconnect to be discovered. It is critical to evangelism that Cultural Christians realize (for themselves) the difference between gospel belief and generic theism. "There is a god who loves me" is *not* the same as "God has made this Jesus, whom you crucified, both Lord and Messiah" (Acts 2:36).

Regarding Easter, Paul used it as the apologetic to make the case for Jesus being the Messiah (1 Cor. 15:1–8). The resurrection of Christ is the one event that turned the disciples from being dejected and ashamed of their association with Him (Luke 24:21) to willing to die as martyrs because they were convinced He was the Christ. Only one detail changed and that was an empty tomb three days after Jesus had died and was buried, because He had risen from the grave and was alive. The belief in the historical event of the resurrection is what led early Christians to their deaths by refusing to deny Jesus as the Christ and is the reason missionaries go to the ends of the earth to preach His gospel.

But for many Cultural Christians it's the reason to dress extra nice and make it to church. It's important, but it's seen as an isolated formality. It's the reason underage drinking is "warranted" on Saturday and Monday, but seen as irreverent on Sunday. Your friends and family may make much of Easter and then get back to business as usual, where Jesus and His gospel are about as significant as the ministry of St. Patrick is to the local Irish-themed pub. We can be frustrated with the disconnect, or see it as the greatest opening available to share the gospel and challenge one's generic faith.

If you can't have a conversation about the bizarre celebration of Easter with your uncle who isn't an atheist but is indifferent about following the Christ He agrees rose from the grave, you may never be able to have a gospel conversation elsewhere. Cultural Christians have opened the door for the gospel to be shared over the Christian holidays without even realizing it. If we truly care about their understanding of Christ, and their souls, we will "talk religion" over the family meal, regardless of what the cultural rules of dinner etiquette may suggest.

Questions for
Discussion and Reflection

- A Christmas-and-Easter Christian mistakes the true gospel for observance, sentimentality, and tradition. Are you tempted to dismiss the life-altering realities of Christmas and Easter and embrace only the warm feelings they bring? *No*

- How should you be changed daily by the fact that Jesus *Live for* came to earth, lived a perfect life on your behalf, and *Jesus every* defeated death to buy your pardon?   *day of the year*

Remind yourself: All of Scripture points to Jesus, the only Son of God who became a man (Christmas) and the ever-sufficient sacrifice for our sins who overcame the grave (Easter). He enables us to be reconciled to God now and forever. Christmas and Easter change everything.

You keep people with how you get them.

It is important for the church to reflect on how to have an important worship service

A tension is express there. How do we maximize the seasons when people expect it?

Making Decisions vs. Making Disciples:

Why Raised Hands and Sinner's Prayers Don't Necessarily Indicate Salvation

Many a good man in his own esteem has been a very devil in
God's eyes; many a pious soul in the esteem of the church has
been nothing but rottenness in the esteem of God.
—CHARLES SPURGEON

Each summer, our church staff has a lighthearted laugh at what
we call the "VBS Tour." We are referring to parents who, week by
week, drop their children off at a different church Vacation Bible
School around the city. I am thankful those children get that
much exposure to the Bible during the summer, but we're always
amused at how parents take advantage of the glorified (free!)
daycare arrangement. While we get a laugh out of the culture of
summer VBS, we are glad to be a stop on the tour because we

know the children will hear the gospel and it will allow us time to interact with their parents who may not have a church home. Our first goal (in an earthly sense, not an ultimate sense) is for the children to have an enjoyable time at church, hopefully seeing it as a place they want to be, rather than a recipe for boredom. We have many volunteers who commit their entire week and even take vacation time from work in order to teach about God's love to the children as they instruct them in biblical truth. We set out to make it a great experience for the kids and we hope to set some sort of foundation they might not be getting at home, or come alongside Christian parents in creating opportunities for conversations based on what their sons and daughters learned during the week at VBS.

We are also very careful.

False conversions are run-of-the-mill at Vacation Bible School and we don't want to contribute to the problem. This is not to say real conversions can't happen there. I have a pastor friend and mentor who became a Christian by understanding the gospel and trusting in Christ during VBS when he was a young child and has now been a pastor for more than forty years. I certainly believe true conversions happen at VBS and are consistent with Jesus saying of children that "the kingdom of heaven belongs to such as these" (Matt. 19:14). I know of churches practicing a strong follow-up process and making sure children who made VBS decisions actually made an informed decision to believe the gospel and were not just wanting to go some place that sounds really great called "heaven."

There are other stories, however, and these are too common, where a child essentially agreed that he didn't want to miss out on going to heaven where his grandparents are and then repeated a prayer after the pastor, was counted as one of the many "decisions" to be reported, was baptized that Sunday, and declared "saved."

The Sinner's Prayer and Salvation

Many pastors could tell you there is a regular conversation that occurs with young adults looking back on childhood experiences in the church. It is not uncommon for people to approach their pastor and ask whether or not they were actually "saved" when they prayed a prayer as children at VBS and were baptized. It isn't the job of any Christian to function as a judge of others' salvation. Instead, I ask questions about the fruit in their lives concerning belief since their childhood prayer and baptism, while gently acknowledging they very well could've been born again as a child in the moment they described. Oftentimes, though, these people conclude that it wasn't their own decision and that it was more "just what you did at VBS." To put it differently, they describe a rite of passage that can lead into Cultural Christianity and, sadly, keep someone there. No pastor or VBS volunteer would ever admit to coercing a decision for Christ by a child, but the evidence is often present.

My friend was a children's minister at a Baptist church, and one of her greatest responsibilities of the year was organizing and leading VBS. After a week of teaching Bible stories, singing songs, making crafts, and playing games, she was thrilled to have had a successful run. As is a tradition for most churches, on the last day of VBS, they closed out with a large group time where parents would attend with their child to see the songs they sang and get a recap of the week. My friend, as the children's minister, was asked to give an invitation where the children would have the opportunity to "ask Jesus into their heart." To her excitement, several kids indicated they wanted to follow Jesus by raising their hands when given the opportunity. She gave instructions for following up and got the information she needed from each child and then walked off the stage as the singers came back up front to lead the families in a silly VBS song from the week.

As my friend walked off stage, she was pulled aside by the senior pastor, who looked unhappy. He didn't beat around the bush and immediately told her "there were not enough kids who made decisions during the invitation." The pastor declared that he was going to go up on stage after the songs and "redo it." He went up on stage, asked the kids if they wanted to go to heaven when they died, and asked them to repeat after him a prayer known as "the sinner's prayer," where the kids asked Jesus into their hearts. Every kid in the sanctuary repeated the words. He walked off stage happily and reported the number of decisions that were made for Christ to the congregation that Sunday morning, doubling the number of people baptized that year in one Sunday.

Yikes. Yes, we should absolutely praise God for childhood conversions! Jesus clearly welcomed the children to come to Him, and I want to join the angels in rejoicing over even one sinner who repents (Luke 15:7). But the question must be asked: What does it actually mean to come to Jesus? Certainly some of those children from that VBS room will follow Jesus from the point of their prayer that day. Like any Christian, they will have their times of temptations and struggles, but I have no doubt there are people following Jesus to this day who would attribute their conversion to VBS.

There are others, though, who were manipulated. Why would someone want to manipulate a child into making a decision for Christ? There are at least two reasons: *theological pragmatism* and *accolades*.

Pointing People to Christ, Not Heaven

In his book, *The King Jesus Gospel*, Scot McKnight urges the
church to consider that the most important question to ask today
is "What is the gospel?" McKnight writes, "Most of evangelism
today is obsessed with getting someone to make a decision; the
apostles, however, were obsessed with making disciples."[1] In his
review of this book, Trevin Wax notes that McKnight believes this
approach is a "lopsided understanding of Christianity [that] is
actually *keeping* [the church] from making disciples."[2] McKnight
would clearly not have enjoyed the "redo" invitation from VBS as
he added that "focusing youth events, retreats, and programs on
persuading people to make a decision disarms the gospel, distorts
numbers, and diminishes the significance of discipleship."[3]

There is certainly an element of persuasion to sharing the
gospel and even pleas that take place in the Bible (2 Cor. 5:20),
but these are calls for others to believe the gospel and be reconciled to God, to know and follow Christ—not only to a moment
of decision. The "preferred Method of Persuasion and the gospel
are not one and the same,"[4] writes McKnight, as "methods shift
and conform to the needs of the evangelist and the audience."[5] For
instance, "Do you want to go to heaven when you die?" is not the
gospel, but might be the most common line of persuasion used
with children. All one has to do is attend a funeral to understand
that almost everyone believes in some place called heaven.

Similar to St. Patrick's Day no longer being about St. Patrick,
the modern view of heaven has little to do with Jesus. It is a generic "better place" somewhere in the sky. That might work fine
for a therapeutic sentimentality during a difficult time, but it is
not the heaven of the Bible, where the point and primary focus
is the eternal worship of the Lord Jesus Christ. Understanding

this helps form the proper approach when sharing the gospel and calling for a decision—we are pointing people to Christ, not to heaven. Unless someone is an atheist, there is a high probability he believes he is going to heaven when he dies. The most foundational belief of Cultural Christianity, outside of theism, is that "good people go to heaven." A gospel presentation that makes heaven the point of the decision is a Cultural Christian gospel one might not even realize they are presenting. Let us not be churches that forego true discipleship in favor of "hands raised" during an invitation.

This is a sensitive matter for many, because "praying the sinner's prayer" is often viewed as the magic key to salvation, along with an altar call or a raised hand. These rites of passage can provide a false assurance, since God never promised to give salvation to someone because they prayed a certain prayer. Rather, the Bible shows that those are saved from sin and reconciled to God who repent and believe the gospel. The vehicle, then, is an interaction between God and ourselves of repentance and belief, but we need to be careful since, as J. D. Greear stated, "over-emphasizing the prayer has often (though unintentionally) obscured the primary instruments for laying hold of salvation: repentance and faith."[6] Gospel presentations must point people to God's holiness, the consequences of sin, the forgiveness needed, and reconciliation that is only possible for those who believe the gospel by faith. The greatest human need is not heaven with Grandma, but forgiveness. We need to be saved from God, by God, to a relationship with God that is expressed in the worship of Jesus Christ. If a prayer is a means to understand that and the reality of heaven is part of what is grasped in understanding the gospel promises of our Lord, fantastic; but apart from that, a ticket to heaven by way of a scripted prayer is not the gospel.

The general approach and method of inviting a group of listeners to recite a prayer en masse is, sadly, often the means to get many people to "make a decision" for Christ. But when Jesus gave the Great Commission, He linked baptism to discipleship. The good news leading people to baptism also called them to believe and follow Christ, not only say a prayer, raise their hands, or walk down the aisle. While those actions might be gateways to gospel understanding, they cannot be assumed as the means to eternal life.

DISCIPLESHIP EFFORTS: HOW CAN CHURCHES DO THIS WELL?

We're not only saved *from* sin, but also *to* lifetime commitment to Christ within a body of believers. This is beautiful. And for a new believer, it can be uncharted territory. It is important that churches home in on caring for sheep new to the flock and make sure they are able to understand the new life available in Christ. What a tragedy if someone does come to faith in Christ and is inadvertently left to fend for themselves.

We also know that faith in Christ is costly. Jesus wasn't looking for crowds but rather a commitment. Three times in Luke 14:25–33, Jesus used the words "cannot be my disciple" in reference to people claiming they wanted to follow Him but who were unwilling to consider what that meant.

> Now great crowds were traveling with him. So he turned and said to them: "If anyone comes to me and does not hate his own father and mother, wife and children, brothers and sisters—yes, and even his own life—he cannot be my disciple. Whoever

does not bear his own cross and come after me cannot be my disciple.

"For which of you, wanting to build a tower, doesn't first sit down and calculate the cost to see if he has enough to complete it? Otherwise, after he has laid the foundation and cannot finish it, all the onlookers will begin to ridicule him, saying, 'This man started to build and wasn't able to finish.'

"Or what king, going to war against another king, will not first sit down and decide if he is able with ten thousand to oppose the one who comes against him with twenty thousand? If not, while the other is still far off, he sends a delegation and asks for terms of peace. In the same way, therefore, every one of you who does not renounce all his possessions cannot be my disciple." (Luke 14:25–33)

So what are some practical ways a church can bring people into the fold for continued growth?

Bible Reading

According to Brad Waggoner's book *The Shape of Faith to Come*, the number one indicator of spiritual growth is regular Bible reading.[7] The church must immediately get new believers, regardless of age, engaged in reading Scripture. According to a LifeWay survey presented by Ed Stetzer,[8] those who engage in Bible reading are more likely to:

- Confess wrongdoings to God and ask forgiveness.
- Make a decision to obey or follow God with an awareness that choosing to do so might be costly.

- Pray for the spiritual state of people they know are not professing Christians.
- Read a book about increasing their spiritual growth.
- Be discipled one-on-one by a more spiritually mature Christian.

Stetzer adds that "Bible engagement points people toward maturity, and maturing Christians have practices that correspond to Bible reading." This must accompany a heavy reliance on Scripture during the church service itself, in order to give as much exposure to God's Word as possible.

Here are a few ways that our church helps people find community and be exposed to God's Word:

- **Serving.** We ask that all of our members serve in at least one of our volunteer environments (Kids, Hospitality, Band, Production, Creative Team, Care Team, etc.). Each program has its own vetting process, but we find that people who get plugged in with a serving team often reap the benefits of deep community and a sense of investment in the operations and health of our church. This has been one of the primary ways our people have gone from semiregular attenders to church family. The leaders of each of these teams are church staff members who emphasize and foster the spiritual care of their volunteers.

- **Community**. One of the core values of our church is "In Community, Not Alone." Another "requirement" that we ask of our members is that they engage in a community group. Like many churches, we have a plethora of small group options ranging from various age groups, geographical zones, and life phases. Although small groups run on a semester calendar (we're in a large college town), we have found that some core groups remain the same for years on end as deep friendships are formed. My parents colead a thriving small group they call "The Varsity," as it was the first group comprised of "grown folks" when our church was primarily college students. It has been amazing to see the life change stemming from deep gospel community.

• **Ongoing Education**. Our church recently began offering topical, open seminars that we call Equip Classes. Members of our church can sign up to come to single-night classes or multiweek courses held throughout the year. We've hosted classes on marriage enhancement, missions, deep studies of specific books of the Bible, etc. We offer kids programming, just like on Sunday mornings, and we love seeing our people come in droves to learn more about the Bible and living out their faith. The teachers are qualified and trusted members of our church family, and the turnout and enthusiasm have surpassed our expectations.

If a church can offer environments for people to come together and learn, you may find that they are eager to do so. For our church, these environments also allow our people to come together and fellowship outside of the structure of a normal Sunday gathering.

Numbers Game

Boasting of numbers is all the rage in modern church culture. "How many baptisms did you have last year?" is a familiar question when pastors are gathered. As a result, there is a temptation for pastors to try to prove their effectiveness by getting people baptized by any means possible. We should celebrate the baptisms stemming from genuine conversion to Christ, but be aware that baptism can still be abused in the name of pragmatism. If we're looking for numbers only, and not being patient to ensure that participants understand the gospel, the ritual can become merely a version of a delayed infant baptism, where an actual faith that leads to repentance is not required.

My hope for myself and other pastors is that our greatest priority for those in our care is a true and saving understanding of the gospel. The temptation to rush people to a decision and the baptismal is real when it is the litmus test for success as a church or a pastor. Yet what is measured as success in the American church is often not even acknowledged by God.

The Way Forward

I hope pastors and church members continue to give gospel invitations at Vacation Bible School and other areas of children's ministry. I also hope children continue to step into the baptismal waters and declare their new life in Christ. (Believe me, I have three children and would love to see them each put faith in Christ and be baptized as those who understand the gospel.)

At the same time, I hope there are fewer people who at twenty years old wonder if they actually became a Christian at age eight. This is only going to happen if we pump the brakes and make sure children develop a faith of their own before we declare them to be born again in the baptismal water. There can be an urgency to share the gospel without panicking them into a decision they don't understand. God is patiently watering seeds planted in their hearts and minds to understand the gospel in a way that doesn't have to be coerced and therefore will not be one that has no root (Mark 4:17). We can trust that He is sovereign and appeal to His heart in prayer that all would come to faith (2 Peter 3:9).

> I can't help but wonder if "Didn't I ask Jesus into my heart?" will be one of the pleas of the religious when they stand before the Lord.

We can't be ignorant of the fact that false assurance exists and that it has eternal consequences. This should pull us away from hurried numbers and toward individual, conscientious patience with those in our churches. Thinking back to Matthew 7:21–23 and my original conversation with my neighbor Matt, I can't help but wonder if "Didn't I ask Jesus into my heart?" will be one of the pleas of the religious when they stand before the Lord. We can't know for certain, but we do know that authentic heart change is the result of regeneration, evidenced by transformation, through gospel belief.

Like we saw in chapter 6, there are some who look to a rite of passage (without belief and repentance) as their own assurance of a salvation that doesn't exist. Please, Lord, let us not be the purveyors and drivers of that kind of false assurance.

Questions for
Discussion and Reflection

- What ways is your church pointing people to a life of
  following Christ instead of to a rite of passage? And
  vice versa?

  Classes
  Bible Studies
  Men's Group
  Small Community Group

- How can you, or the ministry with which you're involved,
  foster a culture that promotes true gospel understanding?

  *Be involved in Classes, Bible Studies
  Men's Group, Serving, Small Group*

  *Good Theology
  Starting commitment there is a
  tractional model of theology
  Impactin the attractional
  so emphasis is on Heaven
  & being decisionistic
  Makes w the center of being a Christian
  Man is God centered
  over simplify*

10

God Shed His Grace on Thee:

Partisans, Politics, and Prosperity

It may be that America is not "post-Christian" at all. It may be that America is instead pre-Christian, a land that though often Christ-haunted has never known the power of the gospel, yet.
—RUSSELL MOORE

Cultural Christians come out in full force on patriotic American holidays. I refer to three days in particular as the "High Holy Days" of Cultural Christianity: Memorial Day, the Fourth of July, and Veterans Day. These are very special days for Americans as we celebrate freedom and rightly honor those who made it possible through military service and sacrifice. It is appropriate for all Americans, regardless of religious affiliation, to be grateful for our men and women in uniform and wear red-white-and-blue clothing on patriotic holidays. But things get blurry—and dangerous—when we mingle American patriotism with theistic language—when "God and country" seamlessly blend together like chocolate and peanut butter or cherry and Coke. We sing, "America, America, God shed His grace on thee,"[1] and goose bumps cover our arms after listening to Lee Greenwood sing, "There ain't no doubt I love this land, God Bless the U.S.A."[2] While there's nothing wrong with asking God to bless our nation, these sentiments make it easy for Cultural Christians to celebrate a generic faith in a no-name god alongside their love of America. (We've all seen friends we had no idea were theists posting "God Bless America!" on social media on these high holy days.) And while gratefulness for God's blessings is certainly a Christian posture, patriotism can serve as a stumbling block to understanding the gospel when the two are married.

Many Cultural Christians see Christianity as more of a demographic than a religious conviction or identification with Jesus Christ, as though it falls under the umbrella of being an American. I say this not to chastise Cultural Christians, but to give warning to pastors and churches all across the country: the American church's celebration of patriotism can fan the flame of the all-encompassing, generic god of Cultural Christianity by not only leaving it unchallenged, but giving it a platform. When churches bring out all the stops in observance of the cultural high holy days, it can perpetuate the notion that God and America are attached at the hip. This is especially true in much of conservative evangelicalism with roots in fundamentalism. You may find, on the Sundays closest to these holidays, that many churches embrace American patriotism so fervently that the Pledge of Allegiance seems to be the creed, the American Flag a holy relic, and the national anthem a psalm.

Judeo-Christian Values

Imagine what Christians from other nations must think about this "God and country" red-white-and-blue Christianity that exalts America as exceptional and makes God a mascot for the conservative political initiatives of the day. As long as our Judeo-Christian values are on display, we assume God is well pleased with his second-favorite nation on earth (don't forget Israel!). Don't get me wrong, Judeo-Christian values—even when separated from a saving faith in Christ—can largely contribute to human flourishing. They function as an unofficial code of conduct practiced for the common good, and they undeniably find their origin in the Bible. Judeo-Christian values in today's climate can be summed up in the ethical portion[3] of the Ten Commandments, being a "good person" as defined by Western society, or "don't lie, cheat, steal, or kill." Adhering to those rules certainly makes a better place to live, I'm not denying that. But while these values help keep civic order and promote the common good, they can serve as a false gospel and a hindrance to receiving the good news of Jesus Christ. Being a good American citizen, friend, and family man or woman cannot substitute for being a repentant follower of Christ.

America's prominence as a blessing to much of the world through financial aid, relief, and military protection should be commended, but it can form a nationalism that goes beyond simply being grateful. American patriotism can take a noble thing and turn it into an idol. For many, Christianity is not only tied to identity as an American, but more specifically to their identity as a political conservative or a Southerner, which are assumed to be synonymous in many places. Scathing Facebook posts reveal

the intensity that can result in poking someone in the idol of
political affiliation. Cultural Christians believe that their values
make them right with God, so an affront to those values is a big
deal. Many Cultural Christians will vehemently defend Judeo-
Christian values, despite some discord between biblical ethical
standards and their own personal lives. While there are plenty of
examples of this in today's political climate, it is critical that pastors and churches remain faithfully committed to the Scriptures
and do not adopt the "us/them" mentality so prevalent in the
political arena.

The celebration of Judeo-Christian values is appropriate if
one is talking about the American ideals of life, liberty, and the
pursuit of happiness, but it is a lousy substitute for the gospel. Is
there really less pornography addiction in the "red states"? Are
extramarital affairs, financial fraud, drunk driving, and spousal
abuse reserved for the "coastal elites"? Is the region two generations removed from Jim Crow actually a pillar of morality that
Northerners should revere? Let's not fool ourselves. Sin does not
respect geographical or cultural boundaries.

I absolutely believe Christians should promote the common
good and general welfare of all people, and our convictions
should certainly drive our political affiliations, but voting your
values cannot get you into heaven, doesn't forgive sin, and will not
reconcile you to God. There are people in hell right now who ex-
hibited Judeo-Christian values,
voted pro-life, loved their country, and got choked up watching
Whitney Houston's 1991 perfor-
mance of the national anthem
at the Super Bowl. Interestingly,
I don't know a Christian who

**Sin does not respect
geographical or cultural
boundaries.**

would disagree with that statement. So the church must stop acting like Judeo-Christian values are the gospel.

The late pastor Dr. Adrian Rogers understood this clearly when he preached, "I wouldn't trust the best fifteen minutes I ever lived to get me into heaven."[4] This means that those wishing to lead their Cultural Christian friends to a saving faith in Christ must point them to the need to be saved from not just their actual sins committed, but also their "damnable good works."[5] Those good works can be the very thing preventing someone from seeing their need for Christ.

Partisan Politics: Conservatives, Liberals, and America's New Religion

I'd like to take a moment to speak directly to the American church. I think many of us have contributed to an unhealthy idea that "Christian" and "Republican" are synonymous. Not all Christians are Republicans and not all Republicans are Christians. Let's just use that as a baseline. When the church gets that confused, we can do incredible damage by wrongly distinguishing between "us" and "them." This happens in both a domestic and global context. Domestically, it causes polarized political divides; it is commonplace for a church member to get more outraged over a political disagreement than they would heresy from other professing Christians. Partisan politics might be the new religion of America, and the church is getting in step with the times. Watch the social media posts of professing Christians and what provokes their most passionate writing, responses, and claims, and you will likely find it to be politics. It is a religion, but its idolatry is masked by Christian language and "good causes." The guys on "our side" become determined by where one stands on the political aisle,

> **Partisan politics might be the new religion of America, and the church is getting in step with the times.**

rather than the adopted family of God defined by the blood of Christ. How many Christians would affirm that they have more in common with a Christian from a different political party than an unbeliever in their own registered party? Theoretically, they might, but practically, the answer is often no.

While Christians should certainly be passionate about making the world a better place, starting where they live, and being engaged in the hot topics of culture, it is usually politics that brings out the greatest passions, identity, and loyalties.

PROFILE: The God & Country Christian

You might be a God & Country Cultural Christian if:

- ◆ You believe that your political party is the Christian party.
- ◆ You would be more offended if a pastor endorsed a Democratic candidate from the stage than if he taught a theologically problematic point.
- ◆ Your social media profile would make one think that God's chief concern is the flourishing of America.
- ◆ You believe certain cultural rights (such as gun ownership) are Christian rights.
- ◆ You believe that "taking back America" is the mission of the church.

◈ You process news stories first as an American, not as a Christian.

You might go to a God & Country church if:

◈ The American flag is on display.

◈ Your pastor implies that failure to vote is a sin or that winning an election is saving America.

◈ Your pastor interprets Bible verses about Israel as if they are about America.

◈ Your pastor implies that Jesus' "shining city on a hill" is America.

◈ Your congregation remembers the 1950s as a golden era.

◈ The congregation applauds more for soldiers than missionaries.

◈ You think "Happy Holidays" is a war on Christianity.

I sat down with a friend to share the gospel and his push-back was shocking to me. "Do I have to become a Republican if I become a Christian? I don't know if I can do that." That was his objection. I'd just shared with him about the virgin-born Son of God, who lived a perfect and sinless life, died a substitutionary death in the place of sinners, was buried, rose from the grave three days later, ascended into heaven, and is coming back one day. "Do I have to be a Republican?" Seriously, man, that's your biggest hang-up? I paused to gather my thoughts and came back with a very profound "Huh?" I'd prepared myself to be mocked for the whole virgin birth thing, and his reservation was the potential that he'd have to become a Republican. Now, if being a Republican was a requirement for salvation, I hope he would've believed the gospel to the point where he watched Fox News 24/7 and got a life-sized Ronald Reagan cardboard figure for his office. But our Savior, the first-century Nazarene, didn't give explicit mandates regarding twenty-first century American political affiliations.

As I finally got back on track, still mortified that he would be so confused, I discovered there was a reason why he came to that conclusion, and it wasn't because he casually noticed that all Republicans are sweethearts who love Jesus Christ. It was because he'd been taught to think that. His entire life, he'd assumed Christians and Republicans were one and the same. He connected Christianity to politics before he did theological belief. And he's not alone. In some Christian circles, God and country are entangled together into a Cultural Christianity not founded on the bloody cross and empty tomb of the Savior but rather the policies debated on talk radio and cable news. This leads to more interest in carrying out an ideology that is man-made, rather than the revealed truth of God found in the Bible.

And this is not reserved for Republicans. How many progressive Christians see conservatives as the enemy on the other side, while seeing secular politicians as allies and heroes? Sometimes these people are quicker to defend a liberal politician than a conservative brother or sister in Christ. Many liberal Christians hold to the progressive policies they do simply because of life phase or race, not by theological convictions, and conservative evangelicals often think like Americans first in their politics, rather than as part of a global body called the church. American politics always finds us somewhat inconsistent in our positions and policies, because apart from a society whose law was directly given by God, no earthly political system can ever be flawless. Each of us bears a personal responsibility to our convictions, yes, but ultimately to the Bible—not to our feelings.

PROFILE: The Liberal Social Justice Christian

- ❖ Similar to God & Country Christians, but on the opposite side of the political spectrum, we see a rapidly growing group of people who feel strongly about specific social justice issues, but who almost position themselves against the church from within the church.
- ❖ Their mission is to apologize for the Bible, the church, and Christians—and to meet the culture in its fight for choice, marriage equality, etc. The Bible's sexual ethic embarrasses them, and they champion a Jesus who would never impose His beliefs on anyone else and would never tell someone who they can and cannot love. After all, He is love. And love wins.
- ❖ These people often have a skewed, yet passionate, view of the mission of the church. Similar to their Republican counterparts, they believe that politicians and legislation can fix the world.
- ❖ They also have a different view of "us" that draws lines at politics, not theology. They'd give more grace to a progressive unbeliever than they do a believer who voted Republican in the last election. They've become consumed with anti-Republican passions, believing they are representing Jesus.

Jesus called His followers to be in but not of the world (John 17:15–16), and caring about the welfare of our nation is certainly part of living faithfully in the world. At the same time, Christians are called not to be "conform[ed] to the pattern of this world" (Rom. 12:2 NIV), so we need to care about people more than politics. It hurts our witness to the world by confusing people on exactly what is our message and mission. Jesus didn't say, "Go and make Republicans (or Democrats) of all nations . . ."

The Global Scope of Christianity

Globally, the unhealthy blending of God and country has det-rimental effects, as many churches and professing Christians believe an Americanized version of the gospel. The prosperity gospel of televangelists has been replaced with glorified versions of the American dream, in which God is like a genie that helps each of us find our true potential and fulfill our destiny. Try dish-ing that out to brothers and sisters around the globe who risk their lives to read the Word of God. One of my seminary professors taught that, with the exception of contextualization to guide understanding, we should never preach a sermon that we'd be unable to be preach in a different country. Since the Scriptures and gospel transcend time, nations, and cultures, sermons should be preached as such.

When God and country are excessively intertwined, it's easy to see Christians in other nations as "them" rather than "us" or "we." American interests win the day in one's heart and mind because preserving a way of life becomes the unspoken passion. Before we realize it, God becomes a means to an American end, one concerned with individual prosperity and ambition. The outcome is a faith in a god that looks, thinks, and acts like an American. This mascot-god is attached to causes or initiatives, football teams, and businesses. This god wants us to win and is happy as long as we are good people. We must preach a better gospel in our churches, conversations, and on social media.

> **When God and country are excessively intertwined, it's easy to see Christians in other nations as "them" rather than "us" or "we."**

One can simultaneously be grateful for the privilege of living in America and thank God for those who defend our freedom, while not missing the fact that our country morally resembles Babylon more than a "city on a hill." Suggesting that this biblical image for the church could be applied to America shows how delusional we are. We are the land of *Roe v. Wade*, no-fault divorce, the sexual revolution, pornography—we need repentance, not pride! If America is the shining city on a hill, that light needs to be replaced.

God is not impressed with America. If anything, people who call America their home will be held even more accountable because of the unprecedented access we've had to the gospel of Jesus Christ through the Scriptures. The generic god of Cultural Christianity might take a selfie in front of the Statue of Liberty, but he doesn't save his people from their sins. Thankfully, that god isn't the God of the Bible. In the one true God, "we wait for the blessed hope, the appearing of the glory of our great God and Savior, Jesus Christ" (Titus 2:13). That is better than any fireworks show I've ever seen.

Questions for
Discussion and Reflection

- In your life, who is "we"? *The True Christians*

- What is your primary source of identity? Security? Hope?
  Jesus / God

- Can you identify with any of the following symptoms of
  God & Country American Christianity? *No*

  » **Misplaced Loyalty:** identify more with
    non-Christian Americans than Christians in
    other nations

  » **American Superiority:** faith wouldn't make sense
    in another country

  » **Faith in Politics:** believing that one's political
    party really is the Christian party (or that a candi-
    date is a messiah figure)

  » **Irrational Defensiveness:** theological heresy
    gets you less worked up than an opposing political
    stance

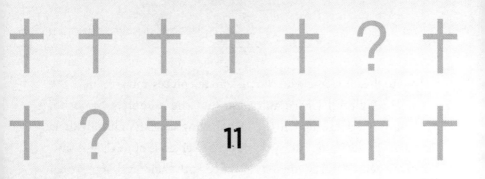

The Moral Theist:

Reaching the Good Person Who Believes in God

Just as the sinner's despair of any help from himself is the first
prerequisite of a sound conversion, so the loss of all confidence
in himself is the first essential in the believer's growth in grace.
—ARTHUR PINK

The down-and-out person who knows he has really messed
up is easy to talk to about his sin and need for Jesus Christ. It
is common to hear a testimony of someone who had a drug or
sexual addiction, hit rock bottom, and turned to the good news of
redemption that was available through Jesus Christ. It is usually
these kinds of testimonies that are filmed to share during a church
service or promotional video for a ministry. These people have
come to a pure understanding of their nothingness before God
and no longer exhibit a stubborn resistance to admit their need.
There is no interest in boasting in personal achievements or social
standing. Their personal brokenness over sin has led them to cry

out to the only One who can pick up the pieces and give life.

In Cultural Christianity, we find the complete opposite. Unless one gets caught in the act of having an affair or having their hands in the money at work, despair over sin is nonexistent, and many people feel adequately satisfied with their level of personal righteousness. People often take pride in achievements and justify themselves through their standard of morality. Of course, like anyone, a Cultural Christian needs to be saved from the sins they have committed, but for this understanding to take place, they need to first be made aware of their "damnable good works."[1] Jesus made clear in Matthew 7:21–23 that works of righteousness, if not done in worship of Christ, are actually works of iniquity. In Cultural Christianity, I believe the root cause of resting in one's righteousness is ignorance more than arrogance. Many Cultural Christians can say they have met the cultural expectations regarding lifestyle, work, leisure, and family; they've always been led to believe they are good people who have faith and try to do the right thing. This may make a great neighbor, but it doesn't save. And therefore, people in this category are in need of true gospel belief.

Common Beliefs
of Moralistic Therapeutic Deism

In the next few chapters, we'll take a look at how to minister to Cultural Christians of various religious backgrounds. But first, let's revisit Moralistic Therapeutic Deism from chapter 3. This can be considered the chief religion of America today. Sociologist Christian Smith, who coined the name, claims it is "Christianity's misbegotten step-cousin."[2] There's really nothing Christian about it, because Jesus Christ Himself is missing from the equation, yet so many proponents of this worldview would likely categorize themselves as Christians.

To understand how you can minister to the really nice family next door, let's take a closer look at the five summarized core beliefs that make up Moralistic Therapeutic Deism (according to Smith), which is one major manifestation of "Unsaved Christianity." For each, I'll provide a suggested focus for a conversation you might have with a Cultural Christian about these beliefs.

1. *"A god exists who created and ordered the world and watches over human life on earth."*

Unsaved Christians are certainly not atheists and would probably mock such unbelief. They proudly believe in God, and could probably share some well-known Bible stories with you, such as Noah and the Ark, David and Goliath, and Moses parting the Red Sea. When you sit down for a discussion with a Cultural Christian, you must remember that this friend probably thinks they share the same faith as you, but that you're just into it a little more. They may have no concept of the difference in actual beliefs. In their minds, they believe in the same God that you have given your life to follow. This allows you to be an ally in a conversation, but keep in mind it can get awkward quickly, especially if they feel blindsided by a theological debate. But, to love a neighbor means to tell them the truth, and that usually requires awkward conversations. Don't start by telling—instead, ask questions about the person's beliefs and allow them to flesh out their viewpoints before determining a point to drive home. If even the demons believe in God (James 2:19), we know that general belief in God's existence is not enough to save, so take the time and care to help guide your friends to that understanding. *Conversation focus: Who is God?*

2. *"God wants people to be good, nice, and fair to each other, as taught in the Bible and by most world religions."*

Cultural Christians believe religion teaches great lessons, can contribute to common good, and helps people become "better." I would add that "love" is usually the primary goal. In fact, part of why they may shy away from your "extreme" version of Christianity is that it can be "exclusive" and "close-minded." Gospel-believing Christians agree that God wants people to be good and fair, but the reason is because He is good, just, and merciful, and has demonstrated this to us through the gospel of Jesus Christ. God created qualities such as love and kindness, but only One has ever perfectly modeled those and that is Jesus Christ.

Some questions for a Cultural Christian would be: "What happens when you aren't exhibiting these good qualities or being a good person? Does God care? Are there any consequences?" You'll find that many Cultural Christians operate as if good deeds cancel out wrongdoings and make God happy. Even Bible-believing Christians can sometimes fall into this Christianized version of karma. But God is not tricked or appeased when we throw Him a bone. And look, I can order water instead of a large Coke with my double cheeseburger, but it doesn't cancel out those calories.

Perhaps we should consider that Cultural Christians may have never really been taught about a *holy* God. It may be eye-opening to explain God's standards of perfection and the sinless life of Jesus. Yes, we depend on His substitutionary death, but we also depend on His life. All people must understand that Jesus not only died a death we deserved, but lived a life we could never live. Any good thing we do, as new creations, we do by the power of the Holy Spirit. Cultural Christians need to understand why the sinless life of Jesus not only matters, but is paramount—their very salvation depends on it. Only One is truly good, and it certainly isn't any of us. *Conversation focus: our sinfulness and Christ's perfection.*

PROFILE: The Good Guy Next Door

Danny is a great guy. He's always stepping in to help his wife with housework and pick up the kids so she can be present at work. He never misses a single event that his kids are involved in, and other dudes secretly hate him because all the wives wish their husbands were more like him. By all accounts, he's a fantastic guy.

When you think of your lost friends, you'd never think of Danny, because honestly, he behaves better than you do. He's a better husband and a better dad. There's no glaring character flaw. Unlike people who feel their failure and need for a Savior, you and Danny kind of feel like he's got it covered. He seems unapproachable for gospel conversation, because neither of you know how you'd get to the part where Jesus is our only hope. You'd never dare imply that Danny is going to hell.

But we have a Bible that includes Galatians 2:21; if righteousness could be earned, Christ died for nothing.

There's a tricky part of reaching moral theists—and it's that your ability to interpret their eternal state reflects on your convictions about the reality of heaven and hell. Don't be in denial about Danny the Dynamic Dad. Denial (on your part, not even necessarily his) might be the biggest obstacle to reaching him for Christ.

- ◆ Do you have a tendency to give him an exception clause because he's such a nice guy?
- ◆ Do you have to rationalize that he's a Christian because he's so moral or nice? Don't let your inner turmoil blind you to his need for the gospel.
- ◆ Are you mistaking theism for saving faith?
- ◆ Are you the judge of who is good? Or is God?
- ◆ Why do you think Jesus died? Do you believe Jesus' death was meaningless?
- ◆ What is the standard for good?
- ◆ Do you believe heaven and hell are real? If so, you can't be in denial about his eternal state.

Fight the inclination to view him as an exception. Ask yourself: If you spoke at his funeral, what would be your justification for him being in heaven?

3. "The central goal of life is to be happy and to feel good about oneself."

The secular Western world is largely driven by personal fulfill-ment. "Do whatever makes you happy. Always speak your truth." This mentality is adopted by many Cultural Christians, for whom faith is not about the gospel, but about the betterment of oneself, or sentimentality, or a mechanism to cope with the problems of the world (for which a generic theism certainly helps). Faith becomes a means to this end of feeling good about oneself, and God is just the genie in the bottle helping us achieve our personal ambitions. This doesn't sound exciting in a conversation, but I must be clear that God doesn't promise us in Scripture that we'll achieve our dreams. He promises He will always be with us (Matt. 28:20), never abandon us (Deut. 31:6), will carry us through to the completion of our salvation (Phil. 1:6), and use every moment of our lives to make us more like Jesus (Rom. 8:28–29). He will accomplish *His* purposes for our lives, but most of the time those are not the ones we have dreamt up.

This is not meant to discourage; it's meant to redirect our ideas of what fulfillment is. Jesus is our peace. He is our life. He offers absolute comfort and joy. We experience tastes of this here on earth and eagerly await our eternal communion with God in heaven. As God conforms us to the likeness of Christ, He frees us from the shackles of our idolatry and self-absorption and changes our desires. It is often said that "obedience [to God] is the pathway to joy," and Christians know that to be true. C. S. Lewis famously wrote:

> It would seem that Our Lord finds our desires not too strong, but too weak. We are half-hearted creatures, fooling about with drink and sex and ambition when infinite joy is offered us, like an ignorant child who wants to go on making mud pies in a slum because he cannot imagine what is meant by the offer of a holiday at the sea. We are far too easily pleased.[3]

Often the process of becoming more like Jesus is anything but "chasing dreams" or "following our hearts." It can be painful, maturing us through trials (James 1:2–4) and difficulties as we suffer for Christ and with Him

God is not a means *to* an end, He is the means *and* the end.

(Phil. 3:10). Through all of this sanctification, we are never separated from His love (Rom. 8:35). God is not a means *to* an end, He is the means *and* the end. What a joy to be able to share such truth with a Cultural Christian. It will be revolutionary. Understanding that He is so much more than a cheerleader or a magic genie will pull the rug out from under them. *Conversation focus: sanctification.*

4. *"God does not need to be particularly involved in one's life, except when God is needed to resolve a problem."*

Following Jesus interferes with your life. This is a sometimes-painful reality for Christians. Not so in Cultural Christianity, where God is always available, but not in a way that changes anything. This god conveniently condones cohabitation before marriage, no-fault divorce, and limited local-church involvement. "I have my own faith" is a common "fallback" line. Christian Smith explains this religion as "belief in a particular kind of God: one who exists, created the world, and defines our general moral order, but not one who is particularly personally involved in one's affairs—especially affairs in which one would prefer not to have God involved. Most of the time, the God of this faith keeps a safe distance."[4] God is viewed as a "Divine Butler and Cosmic Therapist: he is always on call, takes care of any problems that arise, professionally helps his people to feel better about themselves, and does not become too personally involved in the process."[5] A Cultural Christian likely wouldn't admit that he views God as a butler or a therapist, but may function as though God's existence shouldn't interfere with one's personal decisions.

Churches aren't helping, and in fact there is a widespread popular church culture where "the language, and therefore experience, of Trinity, holiness, sin, grace, justification, sanctification . . . and heaven and hell appear . . . at the very least, to be supplanted by the language of happiness, niceness, and an earned heavenly reward."[6] It is rampant and cannot go unchallenged. Al Mohler remarks that we "now face the challenge of evangelizing a nation that largely considers itself Christian, overwhelmingly believes in some deity, considers itself fervently religious, but has virtually no connection to historic Christianity."[7] In short, we face Unsaved Christianity. *Conversation focus: obedience.*

5. *"Good people go to heaven when they die."*

"How good is good enough?"[8] Most people can't provide an answer, but most funerals reveal that it's thought to be an achievable standard for people we like. In Cultural Christianity, one gets to the sentimental place called heaven by being good, so this simple, critical question must be asked of them over and over again to the point of frustration.

A gospel presentation that fails to clearly define God's standard as perfection is a gospel presentation that makes the work of Christ confusing and unnecessary. If good people go to heaven, and we can be good, Jesus "died for nothing" (Gal. 2:21). This is a troubling thought to a Cultural Christian who might have a cross necklace around their neck, cross-themed art in their home, or a cross tattoo on their ankle. It can begin the journey to understanding a gospel that will save them from their damnable good works. *Conversation focus: God's holiness.*

Questions for
Discussion and Reflection

- A moralistic therapeutic deist mistakes the true gospel
  for general civility and removal of guilt through behavior
  modification. Do you find yourself also behaving like
  karma is real? Do you secretly believe that your non-
  Christian friends and family who are genuinely kind
  and moral people get some kind of heavenly hall pass? No

  Remind yourself: the Bible teaches that Jesus is the ONLY way
to heaven (John 14:6), that God is the ONLY god (1 Tim. 2:5),
that His mission is to make us holy for His glory (2 Tim. 1:9). If we
could be good enough, Christ died for nothing (Gal. 2:21).

12

Hail Mary, Notre Dame Wins:
Reaching Generational Catholics

The Cultural Catholic is like an agnostic—offering lip service to God's existence, while resisting his divine authority.
—CHRIS CASTALDO

My grandfather (Papa Tony) was my hero. He taught me many of the things I love about sports, family, and life. Some of my favorite childhood memories were made watching his beloved Notre Dame football team together. To this day, I can name the great coaches and quarterbacks from Notre Dame history. Even though Papa Tony has long passed, I still get goose bumps seeing the shiny gold helmets as the Fighting Irish run through the tunnel onto the field to the Victory March. When I was nine years old, he took me to a game in South Bend, Indiana, the home of the University of Notre Dame. We drove all the way from Florida, just the two of us, and it is still the greatest trip of my life.

After two days of driving, we finally arrived at the mecca of

college football, the Notre Dame campus. Before we headed to
the stadium, he insisted he go down to the Grotto, an iconic spot
on the campus, to light a candle and say a prayer before the game.
This was a little weird to me because, even at nine years old, I had
never seen Papa Tony pray or talk about anything religious. I went
along with it, he lit a candle for me, and I said my prayer for the
football game. After that, we walked across campus on our way to
the stadium and took pictures in front of the "Touchdown Jesus"
mural and the statue of Moses pointing his index finger to the sky
(which has been nicknamed "First Down Moses").

On the way home after a special and memorable day, I asked
him a question I had never thought to ask. "Why are we Notre
Dame fans?" Most of my friends liked teams that were closer to
where we lived and this was a really long drive to watch our team.

"Because we are Catholic," he quickly and confidently replied.

I had never been told that about myself before, and I didn't
even know what that meant. I knew I was Italian and my grandpa
loved to talk about that, so I figured it was something similar. But
for twenty more years, I never heard another word from him again
about his faith, aside from his affiliation with a service group called
the Knights of Columbus. Then, years later, he asked me (now an
adult and a Southern Baptist pastor) a question while we were
watching a Notre Dame football game in my parents' living room.

"Why aren't you Catholic? I'm Catholic, your dad is Catholic,
and so are your uncles."

Surprised and confused, I continued the conversation and
learned that my grandfather was content with family members
and friends who were even professing atheists and agnostics, as
long as they were still "Catholic," but he was bothered by me being
a Christian who did not identify as a Catholic. Twenty years after
our trip to Notre Dame, I sat there fascinated. Another example

of this was about his wife (my grandmother) who was a professing unbeliever, not a Catholic. But at her funeral, my grandfather had a priest officiate the ceremony and conduct the traditions of a Catholic funeral and burial.

Generational Catholicism

Today, I understand that my late grandfather was a cultural or "nominal" Catholic. This is a different animal than Cultural Christianity from a Protestant background. Catholicism is such a deeply rooted, family-oriented tradition that even people who are not believers whatsoever will still claim they are Catholic. It can be almost like an ethnic or cultural identity rather than a set of beliefs.

My grandfather is not an isolated case; he was a very normal nominal Catholic. Think about your own friends and neighbors, and you'll realize this is something you see regularly. A young couple will be unmarried, and have a child. While they have no connection to the Catholic Church outside of their own childhood "christenings," confirmations, and first communions, as soon as the newborn baby is ready to leave the house, this non-Christian and apparently "Catholic" couple will schedule their baby's baptism and go before the church. There will likely be a special gown handmade for the occasion and a celebration following the service with food and dessert. With the exception of Christmas Eve Mass (if it is the year they go to the extra-Catholic side of the family for the holidays), they likely will not return again until the next Catholic rite of passage comes for their child. The grandparents will not care about their lack of church attendance or beliefs, as long as their granddaughter was baptized and their family doesn't leave the Catholic Church. A few years after the

baptism, we'll see pictures of the next milestone of Catholic life—
First Communion. If nothing changes in their spiritual lives, the
confirmation classes begin a few years later, and the child and parents might not be back in the church door again until it is time for
the daughter's wedding, which Grandma will insist be Catholic.

PROFILE: Nominal Catholic

- Will claim to be Catholic before they claim to be a
  Christian.
- Points to rites of passage and family heritage as reason
  for being Catholic, and not to any actual belief,
  doctrine, or theology.
- Rarely attends Mass unless prompted by a family
  member. But, not going to church is better than going
  to a Protestant church, or worse, "getting saved" in a
  non-Catholic church.
- Will briefly reengage once he or she becomes a parent
  by having the baby christened, and then again for
  confirmation and first communion.
- Carries enough exposure to the idea of God to possess some guilt and know that something is off base
  concerning their faith, but often has very little understanding of the gospel. Believes pleasing God is about
  meeting milestones and managing guilt.
- Often has a curiously small view of God (He can be
  easily appeased but doesn't interfere in decision-
  making) with a large view of our obligation to Him
  (guilt).

One of the strangest requests I have had as a pastor was when the mother of a groom asked if I would wear a priest collar while officiating the wedding. First of all, I don't even know how to put one of those on, but that's irrelevant. This wedding was clearly for an evangelical couple, outdoors, and nowhere near anything that would resemble a Catholic Mass. I had known the family of the groom for years and had baptized him based on his conversion and submission to Christ. His Catholic parents were nominal themselves, so they thought it was a nice thing, but didn't come watch him get baptized because he was "already baptized as a baby at St. Luke's Catholic Church by Father Franklin." When the mother of the groom made her request, I looked at her like she was crazy. "My mother is coming down from Philadelphia for the wedding and I lied and told her you were a priest. She might have a stroke if she realizes that her grandson isn't having a Catholic wedding." I laughed, but then realized she was serious. I told her I wouldn't do that, but she could assure the grandmother that I was a Christian and we would be praying and reading the Bible during the ceremony. That detail, she told me, didn't matter at all.

The church where I pastor practices the baptism of believers by water immersion. Several times, we have baptized people who have requested a picture of their baptism not be posted online. This request was not because they were ashamed, but because their Catholic families would find out and be outraged. One might think the families would be excited about these decisions, but the opposite is usually true when the baptisms happen outside the Catholic Church.

For many Catholics, the most important thing is being Catholic. If asked whether or not one is a Christian, the answer will usually be, "I'm Catholic." For nominal Catholics, this is an answer from heritage and family tradition rather than any personal faith tied to the tenets of the Catholic Church. How do we even begin to share the gospel with people who have been conditioned to think that being identified with something is more important than believing it? You may find, actually, that gospel conversations with nominal Catholics are far easier than with nominal Protestants (as in, the starting point is clear and there is an open door to share the immense blessing of Christ's work on our behalf). It may take time for a Cultural Protestant to realize that the gospel you are sharing is different from what they already believe. But a nominal Catholic would recognize immediately that you are saying things about God that go against what they've been taught. Now, they might not *agree* with the convictions and conclusions of the gospel, but they'll know it is completely different from their religion.

CONVERSATIONS WITH A FORMER CATHOLIC

A good friend of mine is a faithful believer who converted from a Catholic upbringing. She has maintained loving and respectful relationships with her extended family, inasmuch as she can control those relationships. She allows the differences to be theological alone and remains an active part of her family while respectfully maintaining the reasons for personally adhering to Protestant teachings.

However, as we know, the cost of following Jesus is real, and sometimes people who are struggling to follow Jesus face the threat of severing family relationships. Like Christian converts from Muslim families, Christians coming from Catholic backgrounds may be treated as though they are betraying their entire heritage. Be sensitive to that.

For the Christian with a Catholic upbringing:

- **Keep the big picture in mind.** The battle is not Catholic vs. Protestant, but rather a battle for our souls to be surrendered to Christ. Don't be combative in your newfound zeal for Protestant theology. Point your loved ones to Christ in all things.

- **Prepare for pushback.** You may find that Catholic relatives are threatened and offended by your exploration of the gospel. Be courageous, humble, and patient.
  - They may want you to identify first as a Catholic, the way you were raised. They may expect that you are loyal to Catholic rites of passage.
  - You can respectfully disagree with theological precepts without scorning the way you were raised.
  - Stay on topic and on mission. Confess what beautiful things about the gospel drew you to it. What was new to you?
  - Pray for them. Pray that you would love Jesus more than your family, and that maybe through your faithfulness to Christ, they may be reached.

- **Stay the narrow road.** You will undoubtedly find theological differences between Catholic teachings and Protestant teachings of the Bible. After all, the texts themselves contain different books, not to mention centuries of different tradition.
  - When you do, lean into those differences and ask questions.
  - Surround yourself with gospel community and trustworthy mentors.
  - If you are being accused of betraying the Lord by leaving the Catholic church, know that nowhere in Scripture does Jesus call us to a denomination; He calls us to Himself.

For the friend, pastor, mentor, or relative walking alongside a new believer from a Catholic background:

- Know that they may be dealing with significant pressure from family to remain loyal to Catholic tradition.
- Know that they may be feeling the loss of family relationships because of their newfound commitment to the gospel. They may be the only person in their entire family who is not Catholic.
- They may be wrestling with years of being told that to go against the Catholic Church is to go against God.
- Be prepared to spend time and effort helping them sort through years of ingrained Catholic theology.

Freedom from Fear and Guilt

You may find that nominal Catholics have never opened and studied a Bible personally, so it can be refreshing for them to hear biblical principles shared from Scripture. For my dad's entire childhood and adolescence, the Mass he attended was read entirely in Latin. He never understood one word, but he was "Catholic." When I asked him if he regularly went to Mass as a child, he told me, "Yes, I feared I would go to hell if I missed." An overwhelming majority of the former Catholics I have baptized were drawn to the gospel because they'd never heard it before. They had been reciting their "Hail Marys" and "Our Fathers," praying the rosary, going to confession at times, and hoping deep down inside that this was good enough. That's not me being unfair, anti-Catholic, or disparaging—it is the truth as shared with me by people who lived it. They carried a tremendous burden they typically call "Catholic guilt."

Then they heard the good news that in Christ, God will "never again remember their sins and their lawless acts" (Heb. 10:17). That "Catholic guilt" became the very chauffeur to drive them to the cross.[1]

Jesus died not only to forgive them of their sins but also to put an end to all of their personal guilt and shame. While the starting point in gospel conversations is fairly clear here, there are certainly barriers to these men and women making decisions to become Christians. In my experience, the biggest barrier to a nominal Catholic making a decision to follow Christ is not one of "damnable good works," a false sense of enteral security, or gospel confusion, like many Cultural Christians who identify as Protestants. The biggest barrier for many Catholics is fear. Not for personal safety, but for relationships and being perceived as disrespectful towards their own family and heritage.

If a thirty-year-old Cultural Christian raised in a mainline Protestant church comes to faith in Christ, his parents may just think their son has gotten a little extreme, but will likely be happy that he's "found his happiness" as long as he doesn't get too religious with everyone else. In other words, it isn't a big deal. But for a converted former Catholic, this can be relationally catastrophic and can send a message to the family that he is ungrateful for how he was raised. My grandfather wasn't serious enough about his religion to make a big deal about the fact that my dad converted to Christ, left the Catholic Church, and didn't raise his family in it. It bothered him enough to ask me that question while watching the Notre Dame game on TV, but it wasn't important enough to him to be personally offended, because he was a nominal Catholic at best.

But many people have Catholic family members who are far from nominal—people who have deep Catholic convictions, and being Catholic is who they are, the air they breathe, and even a greater identity than their claims of Christianity. It is a slap in the face for a family member to leave the Catholic Church and also holds theological consequences in their tradition. Even a softer position toward non-Catholic Christians from Vatican II reveals the belief that, to truly be a part of the actual Christian Church in its totality, one must be practicing the Roman Catholic sacraments, orders, and be under papal authority: "Fully incorporated into the society of the Church are those who . . . are joined in the visible structure of the Church of Christ, who rules here through the Supreme Pontiff and the bishops."[2]

So not only has a converted former Catholic left the most sacred family tradition, but in the eyes of their family members, they are now not complete Christians. You can't blame Grandma, who attends morning Mass several times a week, for being concerned.

These factors obviously carry great weight in making a decision to trust in Christ. Jesus gave some difficult words to all who would be His followers when He said, "The one who loves a father or mother more than me is not worthy of me; the one who loves a son or daughter more than me is not worthy of me" (Matt. 10:37). Many American Christians are not personally confronted with the implications of this verse. But those from a Catholic upbringing who come to believe the gospel message of faith alone, by grace alone, in Christ alone, for salvation, are making a decision that is costly. Hopefully this will be handled with respect and honor, allowing for possible open conversations about why they aren't rejecting their upbringing or disparaging the Catholic tradition, but rather, following their convictions concerning Jesus, salvation, authority, and the church.

While I reject much of Roman Catholic doctrine and believe some of the disagreements are irreconcilable in terms of what defines actual saving faith, I am not going to claim that no one in the Catholic church is a Christian. But I do find it strange that to question the salvation of Catholics is considered offensive, when a Catholic who really believes the teachings of his church would consider me at best an "estranged brother."[3] While I do appreciate being called a brother, there is a reason they believe I am estranged, and it is theological before it is cultural. The Council of Trent, called in response to the Reformation, which convened in the sixteenth century and has never been refuted by the Catholic Church, has some harsh words concerning the "heresy" of core evangelical Protestant beliefs:

> Canon IX: "If any one saith, that by faith alone the impious is justified; in such wise as to mean, that nothing else is required to co-operate in order to the obtaining the grace of Justification, and that it is not in any way necessary, that he be prepared and disposed by the movement of his own will; let him be anathema."

> Canon XI: "If any one saith, that men are justified, either by the sole imputation of the justice of Christ, or by the sole remission of sins, to the exclusion of the grace and the charity which is poured forth in their hearts by the Holy Ghost, and is inherent in them; or even that the grace, whereby we are justified, is only the favour of God; let him be anathema."[4]

The reality is, Catholics and Protestants are not the same concerning some significant core beliefs. These differences are not theological nitpicking. The Catholic Church knows it (even having official statements from historic councils against Protestant theology), so evangelicals should be unafraid to admit it, too. If we believe that justification is by faith alone, we have a mission field in front of us that may wear ashes on its forehead on Ash Wednesday and be giving up Diet Coke for Lent. Many of our Catholic neighbors need the gospel of Jesus Christ, especially generational Catholics who find themselves in a nominal practice of their religion. Honestly, they may have never heard it before. What a privilege to share it with them! The question is: Will we miss the opportunity by incorrectly assuming they are Christians because they claim a religious heritage? If we believe that salvation is truly by faith alone, then "when the saints go marching in" to heaven one day, the ones "in that number" are those who believe that Jesus is not just part of the equation, but the only hope.

Questions for Discussion and Reflection

- The nominal Catholic mistakes the true gospel for religion and rites of passage. Are you guilty of placing faith in what you "do" for God? **NO** Although you know that Jesus has paid for your sin and satisfied the wrath of God, do you still fall into the belief that God is mad at you? **NO** Or that He is punishing you? **NO**

- When you feel these things, what do you do? **Remember the Word of God**

Remind yourself: Jesus' sacrifice was all-sufficient—there is nothing left for us to pay (Eph. 1:7, 2:8–9; Col. 1:19–20; Titus 3:5). It is finished (John 19:30) and He holds us!

The Watered-Down Word:
Reaching Mainline Protestants

Preaching that points everyone and everything to
Christ, insisting upon His lordship and our submission,
our repentance and faith, tends to separate wheat from
chaff and to make the unconverted uncomfortable.
—THABITI ANYABWILE

I was raised mainline Protestant. My family was part of two different churches of the same denomination, only leaving our first church because we moved more than four hundred miles away. I have positive memories from those two churches of the kindness of the ministers and the many friendships made. I can still recite from memory the order of service from the bulletin, which was the same every Sunday. Pastoring in a nonliturgical church, I miss that routine at times. I never would have thought that one day I would leave my childhood church and the only denomination I'd ever known. But my personal testimony of coming to faith in Jesus Christ had to take me outside of my own local church setting to hear the gospel.

That sounds like an exaggeration, and it really is tragic, as I think back to my first hearing the gospel at my middle school Fellowship of Christian Athletes (FCA) club. While there were rich traditions I learned and practiced in my childhood church, I never had someone tell me I personally was a sinner who needed to be forgiven of my sins. Until I joined FCA, I had never heard anything remotely close to the fact that God would not let sins against Him go unpunished—and that I had committed sins against Him.

How could this be possible?

Jesus Christ was someone I was told to emulate, and certainly admire, but I was never told I needed the salvation that only He could offer through His death and resurrection. I was never told what would happen if I failed to emulate Jesus or if that really mattered at all. We had a beautiful stained glass cross in the sanctuary, but this decoration felt to me like the bald eagle for Americans. In my young mind, it was just our symbol. That symbol I knew was about Jesus dying, but why I personally needed that death was vague. I would hear a mention of Jesus' blood every month that had a "fifth Sunday" because on those particular mornings we would take communion and the person serving it would say "the blood of Christ" as he handed you the little clear cup with grape juice. The churches of my childhood had many things that I appreciated and were full of people I loved, but I started to notice that something was off.

The Bible: Historical or Mythical?

"You don't believe Adam and Eve were really people? That's so dumb." I think that is an exact recounting of what I yelled at a church leader when I was in middle school, after taking a few seconds to process what he had just told our small group. If these very first people God made, as told in the book of Genesis, were actually make believe, what else in the Bible was made up? (I was still dealing with the shock of my dad telling me that professional wrestling was choreographed and fake, so this was a little much for me to handle.) The man went on to tell us that he believed the same things about Noah and the Ark, Jonah and the fish, and Daniel and the lion's den. Lest we think he had a thing against wildlife, he then shared that "Jesus didn't really walk on water." I was stunned. He told us that the point of the Bible was to give us some stories to stretch our imagination about God and help us to love one another.

I was a new Christian at the time, but I knew enough to think it was weird for a teacher and leader in our church to tell us that most of the Bible was made up to help us have an imagination and love people. It was also shocking to me that this wasn't shocking to other people in our church! It was a common belief. There were people in the church who believed the stories of the Bible were historic, accurate, and reliable, but there were as many who shared the same views as this particular teacher. These very different views about the Bible existed in the same church and it wasn't a big deal. Outrage didn't exist over a church leader holding to a completely allegorical view of the Bible because it wasn't deemed outrageous. This man was a great mentor to me and actually taught me a lot about loving others; I'll always be thankful that he made church an enjoyable place to be when I was a teenager. I don't take those things for granted. He was a volunteer and gave lots of time apart from his day job to spend time with a bunch of loud and rowdy kids that made up our youth ministry. And, to be fair to him, it wasn't like he was aggressively pushing his loose views of Scripture. In our denomination, those views were not radical. He wasn't using his platform to undermine the teachings of the church as a whole.

But as I started to grow in my faith and was discipled by my FCA leader in high school, I knew we needed to get out of this church. There were certainly some members who held to theological orthodoxy, but not enough to find it odd that there were teachers in our church who saw the Bible as one large collection of fictional stories. The biblical truths I was learning outside the church gave me a passion to know and learn even more. I started to challenge people in the church, and my immature teenaged self didn't quite know how to engage in a way that was the most constructive. But still, something was "off," and I knew it.

"Second-Chance Sunday"

A few years down the road, a new pastor at our church made a comment during his sermon that made that other leader's views about the Bible look like low-fat vanilla ice cream in comparison. His sermon that day caused my family to finally understand the differences were too significant for us to be part of the church. My dad still refers to that Sunday as "second chance Sunday." In the sermon, the pastor shared that it would be such a tragedy for someone to wait until they got to heaven to believe in Jesus, and miss the blessings of faith here on earth. He believed everyone received a type of second chance to believe in Christ. My dad turned to me and whispered, "Did he just say you can wait until you get to heaven to believe in Jesus?" I heard the same words from the sermon as my dad. Being the fair man that he is, my father wanted to give him the benefit of the doubt, so he shook the pastor's hand after the service and asked if he'd meant to say those words. The pastor didn't hesitate to affirm his own sermon and said that he did indeed. He based his logic on God's love for everyone.

Now, as an adult Christian and a pastor, I know what was

missing, but I couldn't articulate it at the time as a teenager. What was missing from my entire childhood church experience was the gospel. This missing piece was not some ingredient or condiment that needed to be poured on top of a snack in order to make it taste

> **What was missing from my entire childhood church experience was the gospel.**

better. It is the very truth by which the church of Jesus Christ even exists. Jesus "was delivered up for our trespasses and raised for our justification" (Rom. 4:25). Without this belief and communication of this belief, there is no Christianity. When I heard this good news for myself and believed the gospel outside of my local church, the first thought in my mind was wondering how I had been in church most Sundays of my entire life and had never heard this before. After coming to faith in Christ, I sensed a disconnect between my new convictions and the things I'd always been taught.

Eventually I realized things didn't simply appear different, but they actually were different. I didn't have a category for this as a teenager, but now I know that my church was a theologically liberal mainline Protestant church.[1] They were very kind to me, but many thought I was extreme or maybe even a little crazy because I believed Adam and Eve were real people and that nobody went to heaven but by faith in Jesus Christ. If someone from a theologically liberal mainline Protestant congregation[2] was asked what the difference was between their church and one that would be classified by evangelicals as a "gospel-preaching church," the answer would likely not be easily articulated. The person may say that all churches are Christian, some are just extreme, since they "take the Bible literally." While certainly there are mainline Protestants who believe the gospel, all across America there are sermons delivered each Sunday in beautiful sanctuaries that cannot even be categorized as false gospels, because they offer no gospel at all.

 PROFILE: Mainline Protestant

- **Practice:**
  - Believes an evangelical Christian is extreme when it comes to faith.
  - Admires the Bible but does not view it as authoritative on most matters for today.
  - Is more likely to conform to earthly patterns of behavior but is likely committed to "loving others."

- **Tradition:**
  - Views church as more of a formal occasion. Usually very traditional when it comes to church preferences.
  - Often goes to the same church as parents and grandparents, and values the heritage of church, though often treats it as separate from the rest of one's life.

- **Theology:**
  - Claims a belief in Jesus Christ, but has little knowledge of the gospel, outside of historic facts about the life of Jesus.
  - Often viewed as theologically liberal, but is usually more theologically agnostic. People from mainline

churches may not be sure what they believe, outside of basic theism. Typically the clergy is liberal.

- Possesses a faith that isn't dependent on the gospel story.
- Believes that Jesus died on the cross, but doesn't believe in the exclusivity of faith in Christ for salvation.

Culture, Compromise, and Theological Liberalism

In 1923, J. Gresham Machen wrote the twentieth-century classic *Christianity and Liberalism*. In response to the wave of modernism that was infiltrating the church, Machen argued that this liberal understanding of Christianity was actually a completely different religion posing as the Christian faith. Machen called this imitation a "religion, which is so entirely different from Christianity as to belong in a distinct category." Growing up in a theologically liberal church, I can attest to the fact that Christianity was presented as a way of life, but not as a set of beliefs. The Scriptures point to both of those aspects of the faith as important to following Christ, but mainline Protestantism usually elevates the ethics of the Bible over the saving work of Christ. Machen explains:

According to Christian belief, Jesus is our Saviour, not by virtue of what He said, not even by virtue of what He was, but by what He did. He is our Saviour, not because He has inspired us to live the same kind of life that He lived, but because He took upon Himself the dreadful guilt of our sins and bore it instead of us on the cross. Such is the Christian conception of the Cross of Christ.[3]

When historic truth claims of the Bible are undervalued, churches will certainly compromise over time, often significantly. In 2003, the Episcopal Church in the United States was in a crisis. The Diocese of New Hampshire named a bishop who not only left his wife, but did so for a homosexual relationship. The Episcopalian churches that believed in biblical authority (and therefore believed in the covenant of marriage, designed by God to be between one man and one woman) were troubled. After realizing that reform was not an option within the denomination, which had drifted significantly to the theological left, many Episcopalian churches left their denomination and formed the Anglican Church of North America, placing themselves at first under the authority of Bible-believing churches in Africa and Latin America.[4]

When biblical authority is neither established nor believed, the only possible outcome for moral and ethical issues is that God will change with the times.

Something significant was said during this denominational upheaval that has stuck with me. Realizing many churches in his own state would be leaving the diocese due to the New Hampshire decisions, one American bishop pounded his fist and exclaimed, "Their God needs to learn to change with the times." I know this, because I was in the room when it was said. I was serving as a pastoral intern to one of the churches going through the process of leaving the Episcopal Church. I learned as a young intern that when biblical authority is neither established nor believed, the only possible outcome for moral and ethical issues is that God will change with the times. Culture, popular opinion, pragmatism, and the desire to be liked or perceived as accepting become the governing authorities. Machen writes,

> It is no wonder, then, that liberalism is totally different from Christianity, for the foundation is different. Christianity is founded upon the Bible. It bases upon the Bible both its thinking and its life. Liberalism on the other hand is founded upon the shifting emotions of sinful men.[5]

At a members' meeting for the church where I interned (the one weighing a pending exodus from the Episcopalian Church), the senior minister passionately stated that the concern was not about sexuality, but about the Bible. As a young man who hadn't attended seminary yet, I saw firsthand what stark distinctions exist between churches with a low view of Scripture and churches with a high view of Scripture. The two cannot be considered one. It is the same reason so many things about my childhood church seemed "off" to me when I was finally exposed to biblical theology. My childhood church leaders considered the Bible a sacred book, but it was evident that their focus on the morals of the Bible omitted the truth claims about God, man, sin, Christ, and redemption. Eventually, a Bible such as theirs will evolve and change altogether. How my former pastor could say what he said on "second chance Sunday" makes a lot more sense to me now that I understand that his view of the Bible would eventually lead to an inclusiveness that grandfathered everyone into heaven. It is no wonder that Machen in 1923 warned that "the teachings of liberalism in comparison with those of Christianity will show that at every point the two movements are in direct opposition."[6]

CHURCH IN THE MAINLINE: HOW TO DETECT A CHRIST-LESS CHRISTIANITY

When listening to a sermon, it can be easy to adopt one of two postures:

1. **Blind Acceptance:** Give the preacher the benefit of the doubt and question nothing.
2. **The Faultfinder:** Look for every evidence that this person is a heretic.

Both can be problematic. Instead, try to listen through a lens of big-picture gospel clarity. What is the point of the message, what is the problem presented, and what is the solution given?

In seminary, a professor gave a piece of advice that has stayed with me: ***never preach a sermon that would still be true if Jesus Christ hadn't risen from the grave.***

So, when listening to or preparing biblical teaching, keep that in mind. It is possible for a sermon to contain nothing explicitly heretical on the surface while missing the point entirely. Use questions like these below to make your judgments:

- Would this message still make sense if Jesus was just a good moral example?
- Is Jesus referenced as merely an example, or as a

substitute? Is His Lordship mentioned? Is His deity
acknowledged?
- Is the point of the message self-improvement or deeper
commitment to and trust in Jesus?
- What does the listener need to do after the message ends?
Anything? By what strength is the listener to accomplish
this work?
- What Scripture is cited? Read it in context. Is it properly
utilized to point to Jesus? Or am I, the listener, the subject
of the message?

It is a mystery to me why many liberal Protestant churches
have services in the first place. Statistically, members of those
churches must share my confusion, as they are leaving mainline
denominations in droves. In his book, *Exodus: Why Americans
Are Fleeing Liberal Churches for Conservative Christianity*, David
Shiflett set out to gain an understanding of why American mainline Protestant churches are declining in attendance and membership. Through his research for the book, Shiflett found that

> most people go to church to get something they cannot get
> elsewhere. This consuming public—people who already
> believe, or who are attempting to believe, who want their chil-
> dren to believe—go to church to learn about the mysterious
> Truth on which the Christian religion is built. They want the
> Good News, not the minister's political views or intellectual
> coaching. The latter creates sprawling vacancies in the pews.[7]

In other words, they are leaving because the Bible isn't present, which also means the gospel isn't either. Richard Niebuhr,

no bastion of conservatism, described theological liberalism this way: "A God without wrath brought men without sin into a kingdom without judgment through the ministrations of a Christ without a cross."[8]

Misunderstanding God's Love, Holiness, and Wrath

Aside from the tragic denial of the gospel story, this theology unknowingly completely misses the understanding of God's love. It is while we were sinners that Jesus died for us (Rom. 5:8). Tony Lane notes that "God's love itself implies his wrath. Without his wrath God is simply not loving in the sense that the Bible portrays his love."[9] Timothy George, commenting on Niebuhr's claim, states that "God's love is not sentimental; it is holy. It is tender, but not squishy. It involves not only compassion, kindness, and mercy beyond measure (what the New Testament calls grace) but also indignation against injustice and unremitting opposition to all that is evil."[10] Much of liberalism is believed and practiced under the banner of "love," when ironically they are missing God's presentation to them about how love is to be understood. First John 4:9–10 informs the reader of exactly how God made His love known and understood:

> God's love was revealed among us in this way: God sent his one and only Son into the world so that we might live through him. Love consists in this: not that we loved God, but that he loved us and sent his Son to be the atoning sacrifice for our sins.

That motivates our loving actions—and our only rational response—as shown in the following verse: "if God loved us in this way, we also must love one another" (1 John 4:11).

While loving acts and morals are certainly good for human flourishing, apart from belief in the gospel they have no foundation; they are merely secular acts for the common good. Make no mistake, there are mainline Protestant churches in your community that are mission fields because they put more stock in the desires of humanity than the Word of God. Inviting friends from these churches to come to your gospel-preaching church is not an act of "sheep swapping,"[11] but rather, evangelism. You are inviting them to a church where they will truly hear and experience the love of God as revealed in the Bible, through the person and saving work of Jesus Christ.

Questions for Discussion and Reflection

- The Mainline Protestant Cultural Christian mistakes the true gospel for a Christ-less Christianity and a Bible that isn't inerrant and is at times irrelevant. Do you ever feel the urge to apologize for the Bible? *No* Do you ever feel the urge to soften its message? *No* Do you fully believe in the inerrancy of Scripture and God's power to ensure that His Word will not return void? *Yes*

- Do you feel that God can be unloving? *No*

Remind yourself: God's love is demonstrated in His giving of His own Son to die for the payment of our sins (Rom. 5:8; 1 John 4:9–10). Scripture is sufficient (2 Tim. 3:16–17). Holiness matters.

Faith, Family, and Football:
Ministering to the Bible Belt

> The most common way to reject King Jesus is
> not with a defiant curse, but a disinterested shrug.
> —MATT SMETHURST

Like many kids who grew up in the South, I played high school football. A major aspect of high school sports are team rituals, such as chants and pre-game routines. Playing football in the Bible Belt all but guarantees that one of your rituals is a prayer before practices and the Friday night games. On my public school team, there was an unofficial rule that only the seniors could lead in the opening prayer as we all knelt under the goal post, with our helmets off, huddled together. A different senior would lead each day before practice and before our games, and they would rotate who led, between the twelve to fifteen seniors on our team. It was always weird for me as an underclassman to sit and hear people who would make fun of me for being a Christian leading our team in prayer. After the game, we would hold hands and recite the Lord's Prayer, led of course by a senior. Everyone knew all the words. One particular season, I didn't know a single senior who knew the very Lord who taught us to pray that prayer. Truly, not one. But this was part of our football team and just what we did.

There was a sign above our team meeting room that said, "There are only three things that should matter. Your religion, your family, and the Leon Lions." This was adapted from a quote by Coach Vince Lombardi. I appreciated the sign and the order of importance. But something that regularly puzzled my teen-aged and still-somewhat-new Christian mind, was that only two of our coaches (out of ten) were professing Christians. Come football season, however, they were involved in the prayers and big advocates of faith, family, and football. While Vince Lombardi was certainly no Southerner and coached up north in Green Bay, the practices of my team were the norm, not the exception, in the South. My high school football program was a mirror of the region where we lived. In the Bible Belt South, religion and faith are traditions. And not just any faith or religion. The sign above our meeting room might have generically said "religion," but there was nothing representative of Buddhism, Hinduism, or Islam in our team traditions. We sang the alma mater, had our pep rallies, and prayed the Lord's Prayer.

In my four years of high school, I can count on one hand the teammates I had who believed the gospel and followed Christ (at the time), but prayer was as much a part of our football program as the helmets we wore on the field under those Friday night lights. There was never a complaint in our city about a public school having a team prayer, or any appeal to "separation of church and state." We never had a teammate excuse himself from the team prayer. My experience on a high school football team helped me begin to understand life in the Bible Belt, where Christian practices don't have to be attached to actual Christian beliefs.

My biggest anxiety in becoming a pastor in the Bible Belt was that I carried some guilt for what I believed was taking the easy road of ministry. I am a pastor in a city where public school football teams pray Christian prayers before games. I have friends pastoring in cities such as Los Angeles, Las Vegas, and New York City, and here I am, able to drive from my house to Georgia or Alabama in just over thirty minutes. On that drive into the Deep South, I pass more churches than gas stations and restaurants. Along Southern highways, there are billboards with messages about how to get to heaven, and big wooden crosses standing on church properties for all to see as they drive by. The catfish is fried, the biscuits and gravy abundant, and everyone's grandmothers are pillars in a local church.

Gospel Access
without Gospel Understanding

In the Bible Belt, identifying as a Christian is a way of life, but sadly, believing the gospel and following Jesus are often not. The disconnect is real, but the Christian affiliation is stronger in the Bible Belt than in other expressions of Cultural Christianity, which provides an incredible opportunity for the church in the South to break through and make the gospel known to a region that is saturated with access to the gospel but not true understanding of the gospel.

This realization allowed me to see that the Bible Belt is a mission field where the harvest is abundant and the workers just don't realize it. To gain an understanding of the mission field of the Bible Belt, one must first understand that it is different than the Cultural Christianity that exists in other areas of the country.

> **In the Bible Belt, identifying as a Christian is a way of life, but sadly, believing the gospel and following Jesus are often not.**

The Bible Belt version of Cultural Christianity can outwardly seem pretty in step with actually following Jesus as Lord. In most cases, there isn't glaring heretical theology. The people know Bible stories and verses, attend church, can say the Lord's Prayer from memory, and take pride in identifying as a Christian. It sounds really close to the real thing, because it is an all-consuming part of their lives. This makes things very complicated and also very urgent for mission, as the differences between "close" and "wrong" have eternally catastrophic consequences.

This reality can be summed up in the remorseful words of the creator of the Christian children's entertainment sensation, *Veggie-Tales*, about his work: "I had spent 10 years trying to convince kids to behave Christianly without actually teaching them Christianity."[1] It is certainly easy to confuse morality with the gospel, but this is a mistake the church can no longer afford to overlook. Who would have thought that *VeggieTales* wasn't teaching children Christianity? The founder, apparently, who realized the disconnect between moralism (depicted through Bible stories) and actually believing the gospel and following Christ.

Turmoil in the Christ-Haunted South

Flannery O'Connor, whose works portray sad and convoluted characters in Southern landscapes, noted that "while the South is hardly Christ-centered, it is most certainly Christ-haunted."[2] As one who is passionate about gospel ministry in the South, I have pondered that quote many times, trying to make sense of how I've seen it play out in my time as a pastor. I've learned this haunting makes appearances at infant baptisms, funerals, and when the family makes a circle in the kitchen and hold hands as Grandpa leads the prayer before Thanksgiving dinner. The name of Christ lingers, appearing from time to time at family functions, milestones, and traditions. The cohabitating engaged couple with no church affiliation asks a pastor to perform their ceremony, rather than a notary, and they have an uncle do a Bible reading during the wedding. There is some unrelenting, nagging pull that can't seem to leave them—the existence of God and that it means something for their lives. Perhaps there is an awareness of the need for redemption and even a longing deep down for repentance.

It would be easy to shrug off my high school teammates and coaches as hypocritical. It first looks that way with praying prayers, talking about religion being the most important thing, and then walking off the field like they had never heard of the Lord whose prayer they just finished praying. But in the "Christ-haunted" South, I don't believe it is that simple. There is turmoil. Not an outright rejection of the Bible in the name of secularism, but a lifelong wrestling with the story of God, sin, and redemption. The land of churches on every corner is a historically confusing place—it's also the land with the haunted past of slavery and Jim Crow laws. The lingering effects still serve as a painful reminder, as every Sunday you can find churches that seem to be as segregated today as they would have been in the 1950s. I often wonder what went through the minds of segregationist pastors and Christians as they lay in bed at night. Were they ever "haunted"? I believe so. We cannot deny the fact that oppression and discrimination

> **Being seen as a Christian can be more important than actually being a Christian.**

often happened at the hands of white pastors and deacons of churches.

In the South, Billy Graham is revered, apologies are made to the pastor when you cuss in front of him, and there are certain people you feel guilty drinking beer in front of when they see you at a restaurant. Image matters here. Being seen as a Christian can be more important than actually being a Christian. When I think of the Christ-haunted South in today's Bible Belt, I see all around me an awareness of God that brings with it an internal guilt you just can't shake or run away from. God can't be ignored, and Southerners know it. But the idea of God interfering with their lives, and things changing if they follow Jesus, is too much to handle, so the haunting remains. It is a way of life that must be comprehended in order to be reached.

Christ-Haunted Country Music

The unofficial liturgy of the Christ-haunted South is country music. A quick look at the lyrics of some beloved music of the South reveals a people who "want enough of Christ to be identified with him but not enough to be seriously inconvenienced."[3] Country music is largely considered to be relatable and nostalgic, but the lyrics can be somewhat bizarre. Most individual albums cover a range of topics such as coming of age, summertime memories, breaking up with a girlfriend or boyfriend, driving down dirt roads, drinking beer, and of course the expected shout-outs to Jesus and thoughts about heaven. At country concerts, you'll see moms in their forties wearing short skirts and boots, holding beer high in the air with one hand and their cowboy hat in another, singing at the top of their lungs about drinking and cheating, followed by a song about heaven.

Country singer Zac Brown, in his song "No Hurry," sings about being imperfect and not being in any hurry to get to heaven. He acknowledges that "there'll be hell to pay"[4] for his lifestyle when he stands before the angels, but it doesn't seem to matter much to him for the foreseeable future. Brown will play this song in front of a sold-out arena on a Saturday night, full of people (who will try to make it to the later service at their church the next morning if they aren't too hungover) singing about a place called heaven that is so insignificant the writer has no longing to be there. In this song, one's actions don't matter too much, because after all, heaven knows you aren't perfect. In the meantime, raise a little Cain and get to heaven eventually. Notice, though, the haunting that creeps into the thought process of the song. Brown knows he will stand before his Maker one day. In the song there is some sort of "hell" he believes he has to pay, and the people are singing about this along with him. He knows something is coming in some sense and that he's accountable. There is no redemption offered, just some sort of criteria to make it to heaven, which he isn't in a hurry to experience. With that view of God and judgment, I wouldn't be in a hurry either.

For another view, we can look into Miranda Lambert's understanding of her relationship with God in the song "Heart Like Mine," where Lambert sings that Jesus will "make a toast to [her] coming home."[5] In the chorus, she insists that Jesus would get along with her very well because He understands her heart.

While the imagery is certainly fun to imagine, the entire song goes into her belief that her choices and lifestyle won't mean much, because she has a good heart, and Jesus apparently agrees

with her assessment. The haunting here is certainly an awareness of Jesus as more than a man. She sings about Jesus healing
the blind and being the one whose face we'll see in heaven. In the
song, Lambert is clearly aware of the reality of heaven and Jesus,
but not of judgment or the significance of sin.

According to the song, her lifestyle doesn't have to conform
to Christian ideals because basically Jesus would think she is fun
and they would get along "just fine." Common in the South is a
belief in God without a holy fear of God. But yet there remains
fear in some sense—that inconvenient understanding that what
God thinks actually matters, so people must rationalize their
lifestyle by attaching it to Jesus. So much of Southern flourishing
relies on God's thumbs-up that many have constructed a god that
looks more like the Marlboro man than a first century Nazarene.

PROFILE: The Bible Belt Christian

The Cultural Christian living in the Bible Belt doesn't have a theological hang-up prohibiting them from following Jesus. They have
an issue with surrender and obedience.

Amanda sang at church in high school. She believes in Jesus.
She intended on saving sex for marriage and being a good Southern housewife. Then she got to college and saw that a lifestyle like
that just wasn't "realistic." *Everyone does normal things like hook
up, drink before the legal age, and live with serious boyfriends before
getting engaged.* None of her previous theological beliefs changed,
she just counted the cost of following Jesus and decided it didn't
align with the real world. So she lives in the tension of trying

to make her "normal" lifestyle reconcile internally to what she knows to be true of God.

Dave knows that his drinking would have to be curtailed if he were to be more serious about his faith. He knows he'd have to explain to the guys why he probably shouldn't be going to their favorite clubs anymore and he'd have to explain to Amanda that he loves her, but unless they get married, they shouldn't be living together. He knows the social implications of a radical lifestyle change. And it's a change he does not want to make. He likes his life, his friends, his comfort, and can't understand why a loving God would really want him to give it all up.

The Southern Dilemma: I believe in Jesus, but truly surrendering to Him would interfere with my life.

Heart check:

- Is there anything in my life that I know to be contrary to a biblical ethic?

    - Fill in the blank: I am willing to follow Jesus, unless it interferes with _____.

- List potential consequences of surrendering to Christ.

- List potential consequences of NOT surrendering to Christ.

- Is there a biblical mandate that I secretly believe is unfair for God to ask of people?

Kenny Chesney unknowingly gives a presentation of the Bible Belt gospel in his song "Everybody Wants to Go to Heaven."

Chesney sings that the "preacher told me last Sunday morning, 'Son, you better start living right.'" The preacher goes on to imply that if you want to hear your name called at the pearly gates, you need to get your act together. The singer refers to throwing an extra twenty in the offering basket to cover some indiscretions, and pleads that he's not quite ready to stand before his Maker, because "nobody wanna go now."[6]

Chesney's description of this feeling reminds me of one of my favorite moments as a pastor—the day I had the opportunity to baptize my friend Brian.[7] I have known Brian for most of my life, and he is what you would call a "country boy." Brian is a hard worker, loves fishing and hunting, and would actually give you the shirt off his back. He's been that way as long as I can remember. He has always been very moral, with good manners, like many Southern men. He could drink a lot of beer and be a little wild with his buddies, but he's one of those guys that everyone generally likes. It's hard to think of anything bad to say about him. His grandparents were Christians and active church members in Virginia, and he would often mention memories of going to church with them as a kid. In spiritual conversations, Brian would always center on being a good person who believed in God as the "big man upstairs." He'd often say, "I need to get to church, man" when he'd see me, but it seemed to be more of an obligation when your friend is a pastor. I never saw him on a Sunday morning.

Brian's gospel was like Kenny Chesney's song—try to be a good person, get to church at some point, and one day go to heaven. But then something happened in Brian's life. His girlfriend became pregnant. In the South, it is still commonplace to believe it is a good thing for one's kids to be in church. I looked out from the pulpit on a Sunday morning and saw Brian and his girlfriend, Allison, in the front row. I felt so much joy and excitement, and went down and hugged him after the service. I met his girlfriend, and over the next weeks and months I saw them sitting together every Sunday, hearing of their need for a Savior. They heard that Jesus was that Savior, who died for their sins. Brian and Allison believed this good news, gave their lives to Jesus, and made a decision shortly after conversion to be baptized and then to

> **Brian's gospel was like Kenny Chesney's song—try to be a good person, get to church at some point, and one day go to heaven.**

get married. I officiated their wedding, and their daughter (who had been the impetus to bring them to church) was the flower girl.

The mentality of "having to get to church" when you have kids in the South was what God used to bring them to Himself. What a great picture of our God. In ministering to the Bible Belt, don't fight against the Christ-haunting culture of the South—use it as a means to preach Christ.

Brian's story reminds me of the Christ-haunted culture in Chesney's song. We see a works-based understanding of salvation, a belief in some sort of penance, and a love for the desires of the world. During this time "having fun down here," there is still an awareness that something is wrong and missing. The writer feels the need to either make amends or not be judged by the pastor. If only Chesney knew that there was a Mediator who could actually make him right before God.

Religion without Repentance

These songs are a snapshot of Bible Belt culture and belief, joining hundreds of others as anthems to be sung proudly by a population that thinks all good old boys are going to heaven, that God knows their hearts, likes what He sees, and seems to be okay with their choices. They sense that something needs to be done to get right with God, but all they can do is cross their fingers and toss another twenty in the plate. What is missing in these songs, what is missing in the lives of these Christ-haunted people, is repentance. A gospel that shares the need for repentance and the freedom it brings can be the key to unlocking ministry need in the South.

Christianity as merely a family tradition only requires maintaining the tradition. It is done through family prayer and sitting together at holiday church services. You don't need the gospel or its power to maintain religious traditions. "A great many Southerners claim Christianity as their religion, mimicking righteousness on the surface while their hearts remain unchanged by the gospel of Jesus."[8] The reality of God is ever-present, haunting them, but not in a manner that leads to change. The disconnect lies in the difference between believing in a person named Jesus Christ and actually being "in Christ." It is *in Christ* that one is a new creation (2 Cor. 5:17). "He has saved us and called us with a holy calling, not according to our works, but according to his own purpose and grace, which was given to us *in Christ Jesus* before time began" (2 Tim. 1:9, emphasis added). Christians are loved by God with the inseparable love of God that is *in Christ Jesus* our Lord (Rom. 8:39). What does it mean to be "in Christ"? Martin Luther stated, "Christ and I must be so closely attached that He lives in me and I in Him." This only happens through our union with Christ that takes place in salvation, as to be united to Christ is what it means to be saved. Cultural Christians in the Bible Belt (and elsewhere) need to understand that believing Jesus existed is not the same as actually knowing Jesus and being in Christ.

Sadly, many people in the Bible Belt are haunted by the idea of

Christ, while not understanding His love for them. The judgment of God lingers in their minds. Believing the gospel would allow them to understand that it is the kindness of God that can actually lead them to repentance (Rom. 2:4). With an awareness of God and our sins, but not the gospel, one is only left with country music theology, hoping God

> **Cultural Christians in the Bible Belt (and elsewhere) need to understand that believing Jesus existed is not the same as actually knowing Jesus and being in Christ.**

will let us into heaven one day after we have some fun on earth. It is ironic that a faith practiced apart from repentance is one that actually won't experience freedom. It is always looking over its shoulder, when instead could be surrendered to the God who pursues and saves. The disconnect is real and the door wide open to point people to something better that loves rather than haunts. An understanding of this good news will lead people to finally say, "Jesus, here's my life."

A haunted house isn't as scary when the lights are turned on. The full, true gospel is the light that must be turned on to reverse the curse that is on the South.

Questions for
Discussion and Reflection

- The Bible Belt Cultural Christian mistakes the true gospel
  for familiarity with Scripture and a religious heritage. Is
  your life consumed by Christ or by a merely Christian-
  Some where in between
  themed lifestyle? The blood of Jesus alone separates a
  Christian from a nonbeliever. So are you tempted to
  behave like it is a Christian lifestyle that makes you right
  with God and sets you apart from the world? *Probably*

- Is there anything you are unwilling to surrender to Christ?
  Probably

Remind yourself: obedience is the pathway to joy. Clinging
to sin without repentance here means forfeiting unity with God
here and in the next life. Holiness is for our good (Acts 3:19;
Rom. 2:4–5; 6:22; 2 Cor. 7:1).

The Harvest Is Plentiful:
Challenging Cultural Christianity with Courage and Love

You don't have to bring the fire, bring the thunder, bring the whatever. Just bring the gospel. It will do the thundering.
—JARED WILSON

Like many families, the Saturday night before Easter morning, my wife and I hide plastic eggs filled with jelly beans around the house and put out the kids' Easter baskets. When the kids wake up Easter morning, they run out into the living room to see their Easter baskets and have their Easter egg hunt. Each one of my kids has a specific room assignment for finding their eggs. We do this so our youngest is actually able to find some and is not left behind by her older siblings. The level of difficulty in how we hide the eggs increases by the age of our kids. My oldest has to lock in and go on a true scavenger hunt, my middle child has a more moderately difficult egg hunt, and my youngest, a preschooler, has her Easter eggs sitting right in front of her, under her nose and easy to find. While my older two kids look under the couch and in every nook, my youngest finds her Easter eggs almost immediately.

Necessities for Cultural Christian Outreach

Jesus told His disciples that "the harvest is abundant, but the workers are few. Therefore, pray to the Lord of the harvest to send out workers into his harvest" (Luke 10:2). That call to understand and pray for the need still rings loudly today, and into the future, until every person has at least had the opportunity to hear the gospel. When it comes to Cultural Christians, it is essential that the church understands they are included in this abundant harvest, and they are easy to find. Many of us are standing right in the middle of the field. Taking the gospel message to the nations requires a passport, a flight, and a clear plan. Reaching a Cultural Christian requires three primary things: a *refusal to be in denial*, *gospel clarity*, and *boldness to speak the truth in love*.

Refuse to Be in Denial

In Matthew 7:21–23, we see the self-righteous rationalize good works and religious deeds to justify themselves before Jesus, and He was having none of it. It is not a coincidence that just before He commanded "depart from me, you lawbreakers" (Matt. 7:23), the paragraph immediately preceding He'd declared, "The gate is wide and the road broad that leads to destruction, and there are many who go through it" (7:13). The road is wide with false assurance, rationalizations of perceived personal goodness, and religious moralism.

Something you see in popular culture, especially in politics and sports, is a type of "double standard" when it is "your guy." If a football player from your favorite team does something inappropriate, it is often overlooked, but if someone from a rival team did the same thing, you would want him banned from the sport for life. In politics, people may be outraged over comments by politicians from an opposing party, but give disclaimers or rationalizations for similar comments by their own party members.

When it comes to Unsaved Christians, one has to have the emotional discipline to accept the reality that just because someone is your husband or wife, son or daughter, brother or sister, or best friend, and raised in the same religious climate and church, does not mean they are saved. A major hindrance to entering the mission field of Cultural Christianity is a refusal to acknowledge what is right under one's nose, and that is someone who might know Christianity, but not Christ.

It is troubling that those who believe the gospel and follow Christ can tend to be in denial about those in their lives who are Unsaved Christians, but it is human nature—and I understand how emotionally taxing it can be to admit that a loved one who was raised in church alongside you might actually be lost and still dead in their sins, under the judgment of God. Thankfully we have the gospel, and the spiritual state of that person does not have to remain one of despair.

Gospel Clarity

Aside from human sin, if we could label one primary cause of Cultural Christianity, I'd say it's confusion over what the gospel is and what the gospel is not. It is trendy to claim that one needs to be known more for what they are "for" than what they are "against." While that suggestion certainly holds merit, oftentimes it takes understanding what something is not, in order to grasp what something actually is. Communicating the gospel to Cultural Christians is certainly in that category. What may sound simple and obvious to the gospel believer can be a point of confusion and false gospel to the Unsaved Christian.

> The gospel is not church attendance.
> The gospel is not "be sincere and a good person."
> The gospel is not theism.
> The gospel is not heritage.
> The gospel is not an ethnicity.
> The gospel is not making Jesus your copilot or your lucky charm.

Make it clear that personal efforts, perceived goodness, and religious activities are not the gospel of Jesus Christ so that Cultural Christians can be ready to understand what they've been missing.

The gospel is such good news that we must make sure we get it right. It is the word about Jesus Christ and what He did for us in order to restore us to a right relationship with God.[1] As Tim Keller stated, "Through the person and work of Jesus Christ, God fully accomplishes salvation for us, rescuing us from judgment for sin into fellowship with him."[2] God has done what we couldn't possibly have done for ourselves: full salvation through the life and sacrificial death of His perfect Son, an ever-sufficient substitutionary atonement for our sins. The Cultural Christian harvest is abundant, so the workers must be clear.

Boldness to Speak the Truth in Love

Reaching Cultural Christians requires boldness. It is a different kind of courage than those taking the gospel to dangerous places where the government persecutes Christians, or the secular places of America where one could lose their job for proclaiming their faith. The boldness needed to reach Cultural Christians is one that doesn't fear social consequences. Maybe you have Cultural Christian friends or relatives who claim to be Christians but know there is something different about you. The difference, they believe, is just that you're a little more "into" church and religion. But you have to let them know that what they see is not someone who likes church a little more, but someone who believes the gospel of Jesus Christ. Our own personal desperation for Jesus and enjoyment of His glorious grace can be powerful witnessing tools here. We can't boast of our own ability to keep a strict moral code or point to our religious upbringing. We must point to Jesus Christ. This helps us speak truth in love. Paul says in 1 Corinthians 13:1, "If I speak in the tongues of men and of angels, but have not love, I am a noisy gong or a clanging cymbal" (ESV). We have to reach out to Cultural Christians in our spheres, honestly and lovingly telling friends who claim Christianity that they might be missing the true gospel.

> **Unsaved Christians are as separated from God as atheists, agnostics, and those of other religions that reject the name of Jesus Christ.**

This might offend a Cultural Christian, but if the relationship is already in place and trust has been built, it is worth the awkwardness to tell the truth. Unsaved Christians are as separated from God as atheists, agnostics, and those of other religions that reject the name of Jesus Christ. Mark Dever writes:

God, who is holy, made us in his image to know him. But we sinned and cut ourselves off from him. In his great love, God became a man in Jesus, lived a perfect life, and died on the cross, thus fulfilling the law himself and taking on himself the punishment for the sins of all those who would ever turn and trust in him. He rose again from the dead, showing that God accepted Christ's sacrifice and that God's wrath against us had been exhausted. He now calls us to repent of our sins and to trust in Christ alone for our forgiveness. If we repent of our sins and trust in Christ, we are born again into a new life, an eternal life with God.

Now that is good news.[3]

The gospel is indeed good news. It is only through this gospel that sinful men can be reconciled to a holy God. Believe that enough and love your friends and family to the point you refuse to allow them to be confused under your watch. A Christianity without Christ is no Christianity at all.

Questions for Discussion and Reflection

- Who are the people in your life who need to hear the gospel?

- What steps can you take in the next week to begin laying a relational foundation to lovingly share the gospel with them?

- What is holding you back from taking those steps and how can you surrender to Christ and obey His mission?

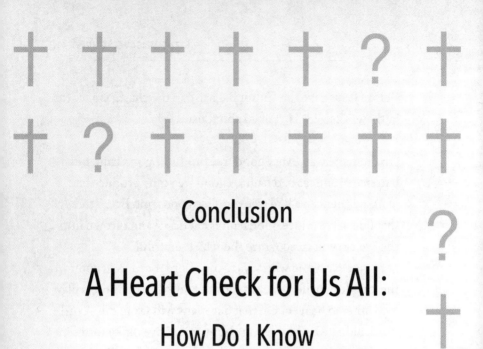

Conclusion

A Heart Check for Us All:

How Do I Know
I'm Not a Cultural Christian?

We are saved by the gospel of God
to worship the God of the gospel.
—FRED SANDERS

My grandfather had a grapefruit tree in his backyard. When I was a kid, he would let me climb the ladder and help him pick the grapefruits off the tree. I probably climbed up that ladder fifty times in my life and to this day, when I see a grapefruit, I think of my grandfather. Even though I grew up in Florida, and was around that tree regularly as a child, I couldn't recognize a grapefruit tree on my most citrus-informed day. There was only one reason I even knew it was a grapefruit tree, and that is because it grew grapefruits. I could only identify an apple tree or an orange tree if it actually had those fruits on the branches.

187

Before Jesus gave the Cultural Christian the chastising words of Matthew 7:21–23, He talked about fruit:

> "In the same way, every good tree produces good fruit, but a bad tree produces bad fruit. A good tree can't produce bad fruit; neither can a bad tree produce good fruit. Every tree that doesn't produce good fruit is cut down and thrown into the fire. So you'll recognize them by their fruit.
>
> "Not everyone who says to me, 'Lord, Lord,' will enter the kingdom of heaven, but only the one who does the will of my Father in heaven. On that day many will say to me, 'Lord, Lord, didn't we prophesy in your name, drive out demons in your name, and do many miracles in your name?' Then I will announce to them, 'I never knew you. Depart from me, you lawbreakers!'" (Matt. 7:17–23)

The way we can know if we are not the people in Matthew 7:21–23, is to make sure we are the fruitful trees of Matthew 7:17–20. Jesus is not advocating for a works-based salvation, but rather for the evidence of an actual saving faith. Even as an eight-year-old little boy, I knew the tree in the backyard was a grapefruit tree because I saw grapefruits. I climbed the ladder and pulled them off the tree myself. What are the fruits we should see in our lives that demonstrate we aren't the people Jesus was talking about in Matthew 7?

Fruits of Saving Faith

A Life of Repentance

John Calvin wrote that "repentance is not merely the start of the Christian life; it is the Christian life." A genuine Christian sees one's personal sin the way God sees it, as rebellion against Him. In His grace, God does not lead us to repentance with a judge's gavel, but through His kindness (Rom. 2:4). He points us to what has been accomplished through Christ for our redemption and reconciliation to Himself. As a result, we should respond with honesty about the state of our hearts and seek to reject sin by God's power. Written to believers, 1 John 1:8–9 shows us this posture: "If we say, 'We have no sin,' we are deceiving ourselves, and the truth is not in us. If we confess our sins, he is faithful and righteous to forgive us our sins and to cleanse us from all unrighteousness."

Eternally Minded

T. D. Alexander explained the eternally minded fruit of Christian belief when he wrote, "Faith in the resurrected Son of God gives us confidence to trust that this life is but the prelude to something more wonderful."[1] Christians don't believe the lie that there is more to be gained by disobeying God than there is to be gained by obeying Him. We know that this world is not our home, so therefore our loyalties are not for this world, "for we do not have an enduring city here; instead, we seek the one to come" (Heb. 13:14).

Sound Doctrine

Scott Swain says that, "sound doctrine delivers us from the snare of false teaching."[2] There is a rotten kind of fruit that can be detected in a non-regenerate person and that is believing, holding to, and teaching, a false gospel. Paul was so serious about the significance of sound doctrine that much of his New Testament letters consisted of instructing the church to make it an absolute priority. He instructed Titus that every elder must hold "to the faithful message as taught, so that he will be able both to encourage with sound teaching and to refute those who contradict it" (Titus 1:9).

Spiritual Disciplines

"Let us strive to know the LORD" (Hos. 6:3). Christians care about knowing Jesus more, which comes through spiritual disciplines designed for growth. Peter wrote to the church that "like newborn infants, desire the pure milk of the word, so that you may grow up into your salvation" (1 Peter 2:2). The first Christians in the book of Acts "devoted themselves to the apostles' teaching, to the fellowship, to the breaking of bread, and to prayer" (Acts 2:42). These were means God provided to help the believers to grow in their faith and affections for God.

Generosity

Jesus spoke with complete clarity on money, proclaiming that "where your treasure is, there your heart will be also" (Matt. 6:21). My heart is far from Christ if I am not living generously with regard to my financial resources. Paul wrote to the Corinthian church that God "loves a cheerful giver" (2 Cor. 9:7). A fruitful Christian loves what God loves, and the Scriptures are clear that generosity is near to the heart and character of God.

Heart for the Lost

Jesus told the scribes and religious rulers who did not understand why He spent so much time with sinners that a shepherd would leave ninety-nine sheep to go find one who was missing. A person coming to faith in Christ is the very thing that causes angels to rejoice in heaven (Luke 15:1–7). If we desire to be more like Jesus, it is more, but certainly not less, than having a heart for those who need His salvation. A heart for the lost shows an aware-ness of our realization of our own stories of receiving the grace of Christ. Jesus said He came to seek and save the lost (Luke 19:10), and if we are in Christ, we will display the fruit of that same desire in our own lives.

Love for God and His Church ❧

Jesus tells us that we show love for Him by obeying His com-mands (John 14:15). But we also see descriptions throughout Scripture of adoring God, praising Him, relishing in His grace. A maturing heart in Christ will grow more and more loving as it beholds our loving God. We also seek to love what God loves: His glory and His church. We see calls to continuously spur one another on to good works (Heb. 10:24), to only speak what ben-efits others (Eph. 4:29), to consider others more important than ourselves (Phil. 2:3), and to do good to all people, especially our Christian brothers and sisters (Gal. 6:10). The Psalms are full of adoring praises to God and the New Testament epistles are full of guidelines for interpersonal relations within the body of believ-ers. Both elevate love and consideration above selfishness.

Cultural Christians bear fruit of this world, not fruits that are driven by belief in the good news of Jesus Christ. They may resemble the tree from my grandfather's backyard, but have never actually grown grapefruits, because they aren't grapefruit trees at all. Let us pray for a true, saving faith in Christ Jesus as our all-sufficient substitute and for the fruit made possible only by the Spirit's transformation of our hearts. Let us come humbly to our God and ask that He continue in us what He started when we first heard His name, knowing that He is faithful to do it.

Appendix:

Types of Cultural Christianity

TYPE	PROFILE	MISTAKES TRUE GOSPEL FOR
Country Club Christian (see chapter 7)	Self-focused, not missional; church just happens to be the social club of their preference.	Comfort; avoiding messy things like visible sin and sinners
Christmas & Easter Christian (see chapter 8)	Holds the Christian holidays close with sentimentality, but the implications of these holidays seem to have little impact on daily life.	Observance, sentimentality, tradition
God & Country Christian (see chapter 10)	Is "proud to be an American, where at least I know I'm free"; digests everything first as an American or member of a certain political party, not as a believer. Can have blinders on to what really matters.	Being American and voting values
Liberal Social Justice Christian (see chapter 10)	Feels strongly about specific social justice issues; compromises biblical teachings in light of cultural whims; believes that politicians and legislation can fix the world.	Advocating social or political causes
Moralistic Therapeutic Deist/Good Guy Next Door (see chapter 11)	Believes God wants people to be good and kind to each other as taught in most world religions; Jesus just so happens to be the mascot, but the specifics of Christianity aren't really relevant.	Behaviors, civility, removal of guilt through trying to be a good person
Generational Catholic (see chapter 12)	Generally either views Catholicism as a heritage or carries significant guilt to be loyal to its tenants.	Religion/rites of passage
Mainline Protestant (see chapter 13)	Generally believes vague things about the Bible but is prone to discard it in favor of the pressing beliefs of the day. Proclaims God's love in terms of license to seek comfort.	A Christianity without Christ; a Bible that isn't inerrant and is at times irrelevant
Bible Belt Christian (see chapter 14)	Displays external forms of religiosity and would be offended to be called an atheist, but in actuality, Jesus has little impact on their lives.	Familiarity with Scripture; religious heritage

GOSPEL CONVERSATION STARTING POINT	GOSPEL REMEDY/CHALLENGE
• What is the point of the church? • What is the point of church membership? • What mission has Jesus given to everyone who believes in Him?	Great Commission (Matt. 28:16–20); beauty of the church; unity of the saints. Jesus' primary call to us is to repent (Matt. 4:17), put faith in Him, and tell the world who He is and what He's done. There's no bench for true followers of Christ.
• Why does it matter that Jesus was born of a virgin? • Why does it matter that He rose from the grave? • Why do you love Christmas and Easter so much? What makes them special?	All of Scripture points to Jesus, the only Son of God and the ever-sufficient sacrifice for our sins who overcame the grave and enables us to be reconciled to God now and forever.
• Who is "we"? • What is the mission of the church? • How would you justify or explain your faith to someone from a different country? Or even someone from a different socioeconomic tier?	Corrected sense of identity: There is now no slave or free, no Jew or Gentile (Gal. 3:26–28). Our citizenship is in heaven. First Peter 2:9–10 is not about America. It's about the chosen people of God.
• Who or what can save us from our sins? Do you believe we even need a Savior? • Who or what is the ultimate authority for what is true?	Point to the Bible as fully authoritative and inerrant; God and His Word should be our source of authority, not cultural whims. Compromising biblical teachings in favor of culture or tolerance is not loving.
• Who is God? • Are people generally good or generally bad? • Is heaven real? If so, who goes there? • How good is good enough?	The Bible teaches that Jesus is the ONLY way to heaven (John 14:6), that God is the ONLY god (1 Tim. 2:5), that His mission is to make us holy, not happy (2 Tim. 1:9). If we could be good enough, Christ died for nothing (Gal. 2:21).
• Do you feel like you owe God something? If you have to pay for your sins later, why did Jesus die? What does His death mean for you?	Jesus' sacrifice was all-sufficient—there is nothing left for us to pay (Eph. 1:7; 2:8–9; Col. 1:19–20; Titus 3:5). It is finished (John 19:30) and He holds us!
• What is the point of claiming parts of a faith but not all of it? If the Bible isn't sufficient and perfect, why pick parts of it to follow? • What does "God is love" mean?	God's love is demonstrated in His giving of His own Son to die for the payment of our sins (1 John 4:9–10; Rom. 5:8). Scripture is sufficient (2 Tim. 3:16–17). Holiness matters.
• What are you hesitant to surrender? What are you afraid to lose? • What do you think is the result of choosing lifestyle over God?	Obedience is the pathway to joy. Clinging to sin without repentance here means forfeiting unity with God here and in the next life. Holiness is for our good (Acts 3:19; Rom. 2:4–5; 6:22; 2 Cor. 7:1).

Acknowledgments

"What do you have that you didn't receive?" (1 Cor. 4:7). When I read that verse, I think of my own life and how the acknowledgments below are based on that reality. I am incredibly grateful for my parents, the home I was raised in, and the opportunities they gave me to succeed. There is nothing I have on this earth that I did not receive from them. I know my brother, Todd, and sister, Sally, would agree.

I thank God for my wife, Krissie, sons Tommy and Ty, and daughter, Sally Ashlyn. Thank you for letting me sit at Starbucks many nights as I completed this project that had been burning inside of me from back to when Krissie and I first met in college. They make me better, are a gift from God, and I am proud of them daily.

To my Uncle Richard for being the first to put theology books in front of me and push me to know the Scriptures more.

To my childhood church Deer Lake Methodist, I am grateful for the congregation's support of my call to ministry from such a young age.

To my lifelong best friend Jaxon Hardy, without a Christian friend growing up I don't know if I would have kept following Jesus. This book was shaped by our high school experiences.

This book is an expression of the local church where I pastor. I am thankful for the staff, elders, deacons, city group leaders, and members of City Church, in my hometown of Tallahassee. They allow me to lead a church that I love and have heard me preach on the contents of this book every Sunday of our church's existence. They know it is my passion, and they have come alongside of me in this mission. Ashlyn Portero and Alex Scott are my local church ministry lifelines. I am grateful for their friendship, trust, and all they do to make ministering to unsaved Christians a reality. I owe so much to them. For all those who have served on the staff over the years, your fingerprints are all over this book. Scott Simmons, James Parsons, Cari Kelly, Sarah Graves, and Lindsey Naitove, thanks for pushing me to start City Church.

I developed a passion for ministry while sitting night after night in the basement of James Merritt, reading his old sermon manuscripts. Thank you to "Doc," Mrs. Teresa, and Jonathan for letting me be part of the family.

Nobody gave me more opportunities earlier in ministry than Doug Dortch, at The First Baptist Church of Tallahassee. I thank God for his lasting impact on my life.

Thank you to the very talented Giana Hall for being a trusted friend during this writing process and for all the hard work in helping me make this happen. This book does not exist without you.

I am also very appreciative of the Moody Publishers team and Erik Wolgemuth. Thank you for this opportunity.

Notes

Chapter 1: Help Them Get Lost: The Case for Reaching Cultural Christians
Epigraph: Sinclair B. Ferguson, *By Grace Alone: How the Grace of God Amazes Me* (Lake Mary, FL: Reformation Trust, 2010), 6.

1. "'Nones' on the Rise," Pew Research Center, October 9, 2012, http://www.pewforum.org/2012/10/09/nones-on-the-rise/.
2. "America's Changing Religious Landscape," Pew Research Center, May 12, 2015, http://www.pewforum.org/2015/05/12/americas-changing-religious-landscape/.
3. Brett McCracken, "The Dying Away of Cultural Christianity," Crossway, September 23, 2017, https://www.crossway.org/articles/the-dying-away-of-cultural-christianity/.
4. "When Americans Say They Believe in God, What Do They Mean?," Pew Research Center, April 25, 2018, http://www.pewforum.org/2018/04/25/when-americans-say-they-believe-in-god-what-do-they-mean/.

Chapter 2: Religion without Salvation: Characteristics of Cultural Christianity
Epigraph: George Whitefield, *The Revived Puritan* (London: Susser-Press, Lewes, 1829), 542.

1. Burk Parsons, "Wolves in Sheep's Clothing," *Tabletalk*, April 2018, https://tabletalkmagazine.com/article/2018/04/wolves-sheeps-clothing/.
2. Kevin DeYoung, "What Is Hypocrisy?," The Gospel Coalition, December 13, 2012, https://www.thegospelcoalition.org/blogs/kevin-deyoung/what-is-hypocrisy/.
3. Attributed to John Blanchard, quoted in J. Ligon Duncan, "Jesus' Prophetic Lament, Part 1: The Essential Problems of Pharisaical Religion" (sermon, First Presbyterian Church, Jackson, MS), June 6, 1999, https://www.fpcjackson.org/resource-library/sermons/jesus-prophetic-lament-part-1-the-essential-problems-of-pharisaical-religion.

Chapter 3: Civic Religion: Generic Faith That Demands and Asks Nothing of Its Followers

1. "Send Cincinnati," North American Mission Board, https://www.namb.net/send_city/cincinnati/.
2. Albert Mohler, "Moralistic Therapeutic Deism–the New American Religion," April 11, 2005, Albert Mohler (website), https://albertmohler.com/2005/04/11/moralistic-therapeutic-deism-the-new-american-religion-2/.
3. Christian Smith with Melinda Lundquist Denton, *Soul Searching: The Religious and Spiritual Lives of American Teenagers* (New York: Oxford University Press, 2005), 162–63.
4. A. W. Tozer, *The Knowledge of the Holy* (New York: HarperCollins, 1961), 1.

Chapter 4: Bridging the Gap: Challenging Cultural Christian Beliefs

Epigraph: Dietrich Bonhoeffer, *The Cost of Discipleship* (New York: Macmillan Publishing Co., 1963), 54–55.

1. A. W. Tozer, *The Knowledge of the Holy* (New York: HarperCollins, 1961), 1.
2. J. I. Packer, *Evangelism and the Sovereignty of God* (Downers Grove, IL: IVP Books, 2012).

Chapter 5: Overcoming Obstacles: Barriers to Reaching Cultural Christians

Epigraph: George Swinnock, *The Works of George Swinnock*, M.A., vol. 5 (Edinburgh: James Nichol, 1868), 51–52.

Chapter 6: False Assurance: Once Saved, Always Saved

Epigraph: John Stott, *Basic Christianity*, 3rd ed. (Grand Rapids: Eerdmans, 2008), 113.

1. Wayne Grudem, *Systematic Theology* (Grand Rapids: Zondervan, 1994), 788.
2. Quoted in Trevin Wax, "Stop Asking Jesus Into Your Heart? A Conversation with J. D. Greear," interview with J. D. Greear, The Gospel Coalition, January 31, 2013, https://www.thegospelcoalition.org/blogs/trevin-wax/stop-asking-jesus-into-your-heart-a-conversation-with-j-d-greear/.
3. Barna Group, "The State of the Church 2016," Barna, September 15, 2016, https://www.barna.com/research/state-church-2016/.
4. Greear, quoted in Wax, "Stop Asking Jesus Into Your Heart?"

Chapter 7: The Country Club Church: How Lax Church Membership Fosters Cultural Christianity

Epigraph: Os Guinness, *Dining with the Devil: The Megachurch Movement Flirts with Modernity* (Grand Rapids: Baker, 1993), 37.

1. Nathan Finn, "The Community of the Gospel: Regenerate Church Membership," Between the Times, July 16, 2014, http://betweenthetimes.com/index.php/tag/regenerate-church-membership/.
2. Charles W. Deweese, *Baptist Church Covenants* (Nashville: Baptist Sunday School Board, 1990), viii.
3. David Schrock, "5 Metaphors for Your Church Membership," The Gospel Coalition, March 11, 2016, https://www.thegospelcoalition.org/article/5-metaphors-for-your-church-membership/.

Chapter 8: Christmas and Easter: Moving Beyond Cultural Observance to the Life-Changing Implications

Epigraph: Donald Whitney, *Ten Questions to Diagnose Your Spiritual Health* (Colorado Springs: NavPress, 2001), 17–18.

1. Russell Moore, "Always Mardi Gras and Never Easter," Russell Moore (website), February 21, 2012, https://www.russellmoore.com/2012/02/21/always-mardi-gras-and-never-easter/.

Chapter 9: Making Decisions vs. Making Disciples: Why Raised Hands and Sinner's Prayers Don't Guarantee Salvation

Epigraph: Charles Spurgeon, "False Professors Solemnly Warned" (sermon, Exeter Hall, Strand, August 24, 1856), in *The New Park Street Pulpit*, vol. 2 (London: Passmore and Alabaster, 1856), 392.

1. Scot McKnight, *The King Jesus Gospel: The Original Good News Revisited* (Grand Rapids: Zondervan, 2011), 18.
2. Trevin Wax, "Scot McKnight and the 'King Jesus Gospel' 1: Points of Agreement," The Gospel Coalition, September 13, 2011, https://www.thegospelcoalition.org/blogs/trevin-wax/scot-mcknight-and-the-king-jesus-gospel-1-points-of-agreement/.
3. McKnight, *The King Jesus Gospel*, 20; quoted in Wax, "Scot McKnight."
4. Ibid., 42.
5. Ibid.
6. Quoted in Trevin Wax, "Stop Asking Jesus Into Your Heart? A Conversation with J. D. Greear," interview with J. D. Greear, The Gospel Coalition, January 31, 2013, https://www.thegospelcoalition.org/blogs/trevin-wax/stop-asking-jesus-into-your-heart-a-conversation-with-j-d-greear/.
7. Brad J. Waggoner, *The Shape of Faith to Come: Spiritual Formation and the Future of Discipleship* (Nashville: B&H, 2008).
8. Ed Stetzer, "Bible Engagement Impacts Spiritual Maturity," Facts and Trends, June 12, 2013, https://factsandtrends.net/2013/06/12/bible-engagement-impacts-spiritual-maturity/.

Chapter 10: God Shed His Grace on Thee: Partisans, Politics, and Prosperity

Epigraph: *Onward: Engaging the Culture without Losing the Gospel* (Nashville: B&H, 2015), 218.
1. K. L. Bates (lyricist) and W. A. Fisher (composer), "America the Beautiful" (Boston: Oliver Ditson Company, 1917).
2. Lee Greenwood, "God Bless the U.S.A.," lyrics © Universal Music Publishing Group, 1984.
3. As opposed to the commands concerning the worship of God and keeping the Sabbath.
4. Adrian Rogers, *What Every Christian Ought to Know Day by Day: Essential Truths for Growing Your Faith* (Nashville: B&H, 2008), 78.
5. Attributed to John Gerstner, https://www.goodreads.com/quotes/99280-the-main-thing-between-you-and-god-is-not-so.

Chapter 11: The Moral Theist: Reaching the Good Person Who Believes in God

Epigraph: Arthur W. Pink, *The Sovereignty of God* (1918; repr., Blacksburg, VA: Wilder Publications, 2008), 188.
1. Attributed to John Gerstner, https://www.goodreads.com/quotes/99280-the-main-thing-between-you-and-god-is-not-so.
2. Christian Smith with Melina Lundquist Denton, *Soul Searching: The Religious and Spiritual Lives of American Teenagers* (Oxford: Oxford University Press, 2005), 171.
3. C. S. Lewis, *The Weight of Glory* (1949; repr., New York: HarperOne, 2001), 27.
4. Smith, *Soul Searching*, 164.
5. Ibid., 165.
6. Ibid., 171.
7. Al Mohler, "Moralistic Therapeutic Deism–the New American Religion," Albertmohler.com, April 11, 2005, https://albertmohler.com/2005/04/11/moralistic-therapeutic-deism-the-new-american-religion-2/.

8. Andy Stanley, *How Good Is Good Enough?* (Sisters, OR: Multnomah, 2003).

Chapter 12: Hail Mary, Notre Dame Wins: Reaching Generational Catholics
Epigraph: Chris Castaldo, "Reaching Catholics in Your Community," The Gospel
Coalition, February 24, 2013, https://www.thegospelcoalition.org/article/
reaching-catholics-in-your-community/.
   1. See Erik Raymond, "Guilt is a Chauffeur to Drive You to the Cross," The Gospel
Coalition, January 16, 2013, https://www.thegospelcoalition.org/blogs/erik-
raymond/guilt-is-a-chauffeur-to-drive-you-to-the-cross/.
   2. Quoted in Kevin DeYoung, "Protestant and Catholic: What's the Difference?,"
The Gospel Coalition, September 12, 2017, https://www.thegospelcoalition.
org/blogs/kevin-deyoung/protestant-and-catholic-whats-the-difference/.
   3. See ibid.
   4. "On Justification," The Council of Trent, http://www.thecounciloftrent.com/
ch6.htm.

Chapter 13: The Watered-Down Word: Reaching Mainline Protestants
Epigraph: Thabiti Anyabwile, "Distinctive Christianity in a Nominal Christian
Culture, Part 2: Preaching," The Gospel Coalition, September 27, 2006, https://
www.thegospelcoalition.org/blogs/thabiti-anyabwile/distinctive-christianity-
in-nominal_27/.
   1. I am happy to report that the current leadership of my childhood church is
evangelical.
   2. Not all of these churches are theologically liberal.
   3. J. Gresham Machen, *Christianity and Liberalism* (Grand Rapids: Eerdmans,
1923), 117.
   4. Laurie Goodstein, "Episcopal Split as Conservatives Form New Group," *New
York Times*, December 3, 2008, https://www.nytimes.com/2008/12/04/
us/04episcopal.html.
   5. J. Gresham Machen, *Christianity and Liberalism* (Grand Rapids: Eerdmans,
1923), 79.
   6. Ibid., 53.
   7. Dave Shiflett, *Exodus: Why Americans Are Fleeing Liberal Churches for Conservative
Christianity* (New York: Sentinel, 2005), xii; quoted in Albert Mohler, "A New
Exodus? Americans are Exiting Liberal Churches," Albert Mohler (website), June
6, 2005, https://albertmohler.com/2005/06/06/a-new-exodus-americans-are-
exiting-liberal-churches-3/.
   8. Richard Niebuhr, *The Kingdom of God in America* (1937; repr., Middletown, CT:
Wesleyan University Press, 1988), 193.
   9. Tony Lane, "The Wrath of God as an Aspect of the Love of God," in *Nothing Greater,
Nothing Better: Theological Essays on the Love of God*, ed. Kevin J. Vanhoozer (Grand
Rapids: Eerdmans, 2001), 139.
   10. Timothy George, "No Squishy Love," First Things, July 29, 2013, https://www
.firstthings.com/web-exclusives/2013/07/no-squishy-love.
   11. This is the act of churches growing through building a congregation with
Christians who have left other churches in the same community.

Chapter 14: Faith, Family, and Football: Ministering to the Bible Belt

Epigraph: Matt Smethurst, Twitter post, November 26, 2018, 11:48 a.m., https://twitter.com/MattSmethurst/status/1067143075531841537.

1. Quoted in Megan Basham, "It's Not about the Dream," *World Magazine*, September 12, 2011, https://world.wng.org/2011/09/its_not_about_the_dream.
2. Flannery O'Connor, *Mystery and Manners: Occasional Prose* (New York: Farrar, Straus and Giroux, 1962), 44.
3. D. A. Carson, *A Call to Spiritual Reformation: Priorities from Paul and His Prayers* (Grand Rapids: Baker, 1992), 121.
4. Zac Brown, "No Hurry," lyrics © Warner/Chappell Music, Inc, Reach Music Publishing, 2010.
5. Miranda Lambert, "Heart Like Mine," lyrics © Sony/ATV Music Publishing LLC, ME Gusta Music, 2011.
6. Kenny Chesney, "Everybody Wants to Go to Heaven," lyrics © Spirit Music Group, Kobalt Music Publishing Ltd., Ole Media Management LP, 2008.
7. Name has been changed to protect privacy.
8. Tyler Jones, "The Poison of Quaint Moralism," May 12, 2010, https://www.facebook.com/notes/resurgence/the-poison-of-quaint-moralism/437270067845/.

Chapter 15: The Harvest Is Plentiful: Challenging Cultural Christianity with Courage and Love

Epigraph: https://www.pinterest.com/pin/182958803589522809.

1. Graeme Goldsworthy, "Lecture 1: The Necessity and Viability of Biblical Theology," *The Southern Baptist Journal of Theology* 12, no. 4 (Winter 2008), http://equip.sbts.edu/publications/journals/journal-of-theology/sbjt-124-winter-2008/lecture-1-the-necessity-and-viability-of-biblical-theology.
2. Tim Keller, "Tim Keller Explains the Gospel," Acts 29, December 12, 2008, https://www.acts29.com/tim-keller-explains-the-gospel/.
3. Mark Dever, *The Gospel and Personal Evangelism* (Wheaton, IL: Crossway, 2007), 43.

Conclusion: A Heart Check for Us All: How Do I Know I'm Not a Cultural Christian?

Epigraph: Fred Sanders, *The Deep Things of God: How the Trinity Changes Everything* (Wheaton, IL: Crossway, 2010), 117.

1. T. D. Alexander, "Be Heavenly Minded So That You're of Earthly Good," The Gospel Coalition, April 18, 2018, https://www.thegospelcoalition.org/article/heavenly-minded-youre-earthly-good/.
2. Scott Swain, "What Is Doctrine?," Ligonier Ministries, May 1, 2015, https://www.ligonier.org/learn/articles/what-doctrine.

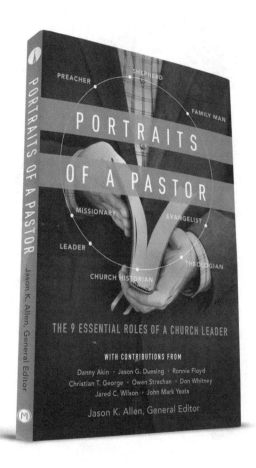

STUDY THE BIBLE WITH PROFESSORS FROM MOODY BIBLE INSTITUTE

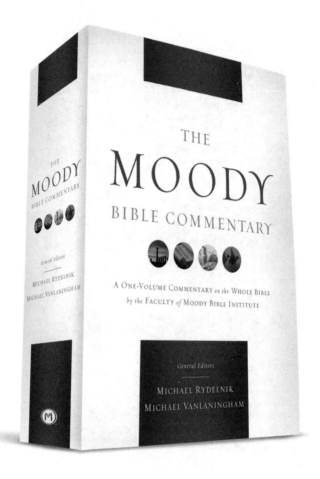

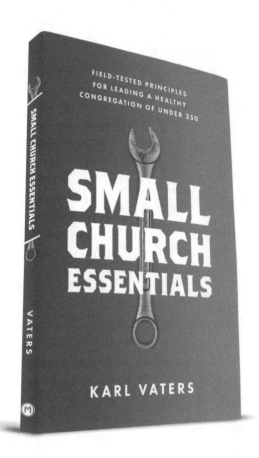